The aim of the *Earth Quest* series is to examine and explain how shamanic principles can be applied in the journey towards self-discovery – and beyond.

Each person's Earth quest is the search for meaning and purpose in their life – it is the establishment of identity and the realisation of inner potentials and individual responsibility.

Each book in the series examines aspects of a life science that is in harmony with the Earth and shows how each person can attune themselves to nature. Each book imparts knowledge of the Craft of Life.

D0731455

The Celtic Shaman

A HANDBOOK

John Matthews has been studying the Celtic traditions for over twenty years, and has written more than twenty books on these and related subjects. He regards his life-time task as building bridges between the native British shamanic traditions and those of other cultures. He was born in 1948 and currently lives in Oxford with his life-partner Caitlín Matthews and their son Emrys.

SELECTED TITLES BY THE SAME AUTHOR

The Arthurian Book of Days
The Elements of The Arthurian Tradition
The Elements of The Grail Tradition
Gawain, Knight of the Goddess
Taliesin: Shamanism and the Bardic Mysteries in Britain and Ireland
The Western Way (written with Caitlín Matthews)

EARTH QUEST

The Celtic Shaman

A HANDBOOK

John Matthews

ELEMENT

Shaftesbury, Dorset ● Rockport, Massachusetts
Brisbane, Queensland

© John Matthews 1991

First published in Great Britain in 1991 by
Element Books Limited
Shaftesbury, Dorset

Published in the USA in 1992 by
Element, Inc.
42 Broadway, Rockport, MA 01966

Published in Australia by
Element Books Limited for
Jacaranda Wiley Limited
33 Park Road, Milton, Brisbane, 4064

Reprinted 1992
Reprinted February and July 1993
Reprinted July and September 1994

All rights reserved.
No part of this book may be
reproduced or utilised in any form or by any means,
electronic or mechanical, without permission in
writing from the Publisher.

Cover design by Max Fairbrother
Designed by Roger Lightfoot
Typeset by Poole Typesetting (Wessex) Ltd.
Printed and bound in Great Britain by
Redwood Books, Trowbridge, Wiltshire

British Library Cataloguing in Publication
Data available

Library of Congress Cataloging in Publication
Data available

ISBN 1–85230–245–3

Contents

Practical Skills

List of Figures

To all the members, past and future, of the White Horse Clan.

Shamans transmit to their people in sign, song and dance the nature of the cosmic geography that has been revealed to them in the process of initiation trances and soul journeys. Map-makers and myth-dancers, shamans live internally in a multi-dimensional realm continuous with so-called ordinary reality.

Joan Halifax — Shamanic Voices

ACKNOWLEDGEMENTS

My greatest debt of gratitude, as so often before, is to my wife, Caitlín, for her continuing support throughout the trials and tribulations of a writer's life, and especially for her work on the material for Chapter 5, for which she saw more applications that I ever would. Without her this book would be the poorer, I alone, of course, am responsible for its faults.

After this I would wish to acknowledge Old Man, who speaks to my heart and encourages me continually to dare further; my own inner shaman Taliesin, he of the Starry Brow and caustic tongue; my spiritual brother and 'star shaman', David Spangler, for being there at the right moment and showing me new ways of thinking and feeling; Felicity Aldridge for her wise and thoughtful words and her advice at the eleventh hour; Robert Lentz, iconographer, who gave us a new set of the Hallows, and sent us on a new journey; Simon Buxton and the gang at Arcania, and William Bloom of Alternatives for encouragement and the opportunity to try out some of the techniques given here. Special thanks also to Jerry Ozaniec and Katherine Kurtz, for helping me through yet another computing crisis. Lastly, to Chesca, Stuart and Miranda, a talented threesome, whose images continue to inspire all who pursue the path of the Celtic tradition.

Introduction
The Shaman's World

'Every one born on this earth's soil is a
native person now and must learn to
live in harmony and balance.

The Ceremonial Circle
Sedonia Cahill & Joshua Halpern

SHAMANISM IS VERY PROBABLY the oldest known spiritual discipline in the
world. Visible signs of its practice have been discovered in Australia, the
Americas, Siberia and parts of Europe, dating back to the dawn of
history. Rock paintings, ancient carved stones, and painted shells, ori-
ginating from sites as far apart as Scotland, France, South and North
America, the Arctic Circle and the Australian Bush, have given us
glimpses into the life and practice of the shaman.

These ancient disciplines are still taught in many parts of the world,
and contemporary practitioners of this tradition add a living dimension
to the artefacts. The world thus revealed, for all its constant overlapping
with the inner realms of the spirit, is at times an overwhelmingly
substantial one, possessing a universality which enables modern shamans to talk essentially the same language irrespective of background or
race.

Because it is not an organized religion as such, but rather a spiritual
practice, shamanism cuts across all faiths and creeds, reaching deep levels of
ancestral memory. As a primal belief system, which precedes established
religion, it has its own universal symbolism and cosmology, inhabited by
beings, gods and totems, who display similar characteristics although they
appear in various forms, depending on their places of origin.

This book is an attempt to suggest the form once taken by the native shamanism of Britain and Ireland. Every technique and exercise can be traced back to some aspect of Celtic life or culture, and though it finds certain analogies in other shamanic traditions, such as North American, Uralian, or Lapp, it does not borrow from any of these. The traditions outlined are purely Celtic in inspiration.

Celtic is here taken to refer to the traditions and ways of people native to the British Isles. In fact, the Celts are no more 'British' than the Saxons or Normans who came after them. They were themselves incomers from the Indo-European world, and incorporated their own practices with those of the indigenous people, thereby honouring the sacredness of the land they had come to dwell in.

The Greek historian Herodotus mentions incidentally the *Keltoi* as living in and around the Danube about 550BC. The reference apparently needed no qualification or explanation, from which we may surmise that the Celts were well established by this time, and had already had some interchange with the Greeks. Certainly they had reached Britain and Ireland by this date and had subjugated the previous inhabitants, a shadowy folk sometimes identified as the Picts in the north of Britain, and as the Fomorians in Ireland.

These peoples left little indication of either their culture or beliefs, though these may well have influenced the incoming tribes, and thus helped create our powerful Celtic traditions. The term 'Celtic' has thus come to stand for a path that is recognizably of the lands of England, Ireland, Scotland and Wales. Therefore this book deals with 'Celtic' (as opposed to native American, Australian or Siberian) shamanism, specifically in its location and in its utilization of known methods and practices native to this part of the western hemisphere. But it is not intended to be exclusively for use by those of Celtic blood and culture; just as many western practitioners of alternative belief-systems have found native American or Aboriginal shamanic practice useful, so it is hoped that these people will be excited to learn that they possess a native shamanism.

A full historical account of how the system and methods of working described herein were arrived at will be found in my *Taliesin: Shamanism and the Bardic Mysteries in Britain and Ireland* (Mandala, 1991). The contents of the present volume are purely practical, and the historical background has been kept to a minimum. Those who require a more solid basis for understanding are referred to the earlier book.

The shamanic tradition of the Celts never completely disappeared, despite long periods in which it was virtually forgotten. Practices such as scrying, second sight, spiritual healing, prophecy, poetic invocation and communication with the otherworld, have been maintained – often in fragmentary form – in most of the Celtic countries. But a degree of cultural isolation has made the tradition's occasional forays into the world short-lived, misunderstood or misinterpreted. We still have to work hard to recover what has been lost; fortunately sufficient material remains to enable us to restore many of the old traditions so that they work for us today.

To give an idea of the *feel* of Celtic shamanism, here are two old stories in which the threads of native British shamanic tradition can clearly be seen. The first originates from Wales in a very ancient past; although the version we know today was not written down until medieval times, the antiquity of the themes is undeniable.

The Story of Taliesin

A young boy named Gwion Bach (Gwion the Little) is set to watch over a cauldron prepared by the Goddess Ceridwen. The brew distilling within it is intended for her son, the hideously ugly Afagddu (Utter Darkness); when drunk it will give him all knowledge, and the wisdom to use it. But while Ceridwen is absent three drops of liquid splash out of the cauldron onto Gwion's finger. Sucking it to alleviate the pain he imbibes the wisdom meant for Afagddu. But with this comes danger. Ceridwen, aware by her magic of what has occurred, comes in pursuit of Gwion, who flees from her in the shape of various animals, birds and fish. Each time he assumes one form, Ceridwen assumes that of its natural predator. Finally, after a long chase, Gwion becomes a grain of wheat in a heap of chaff and Ceridwen, in the form of a red-crested hen, eats the grain. Nine months later she gives birth to a beautiful boy, whom she cannot bear to kill and so sets adrift in a leather bag on the sea. Eventually the bag fetches up in the salmon weir of Gwyddno Garanhir, where it is discovered by Gwyddno's hapless son Elffin. On opening the bag he sees the bright forehead of the child and exclaims: 'Behold, the radiant brow!', whereupon the child answers 'Taliesin be he called' (*Tal-iessin* = shining brow). He then proceeds to give forth an extraordinary stream of inspired poetic utterance, prophecy and wisdom, the products of having imbibed the brew of inspiration. Taken back to Elffin's home he becomes a famous bard and shaman, later serving at the court of Arthur.

The shamanic nature of this story, which disguises an account of initiation and rebirth as changes into animal, bird and fish, is beyond doubt. The initiation itself gives rise to great wisdom, which was afterwards encoded in the poems attributed to Taliesin. There we read not only of his transformation into other creatures, but also his symbolic relationship with the whole of creation. This is a major objective of shamans everywhere, and in the figure of Taliesin and the teachings which have grown up around him, the primary elements of Celtic shamanism are preserved.

In the second story, that of Suibhne, which derives from ancient Irish sources, we again have a tale of transformation and poetic inspiration; but this time with the added dimension of inspired madness, which is also an integral part of world-wide shamanic tradition.

The Story of Suibhne Geilt

Suibhne was a king and poet who ruled over the Dalraidhe. One day, after he had been cursed by a Christian saint, the sight of the carnage of battle sent him mad and he lived for a long time in the wilderness, sleeping in the tops of trees. He wore a cloak of feathers and could fly from tree-top to tree-top. During these periods of inspired 'madness', he made prophetic statements which later proved to be true. On one occasion he had a contest with the Hag of the Mill who fell to her death when she was unable to match a great leap made by Suibhne. Several times, friends sought him out and tried to persuade him to return home, but each time something happened to drive him further into 'madness'. In the end he met death in a bizarre manner: a cook at the monastery where Suibhne's confidant, St Molling, entertained him to supper, grew jealous of his wife's affection for the mad exile and stabbed him with a spear.

This story, though very different from that of Taliesin, betrays many aspects of Celtic shamanism. When 'mad' or 'inspired', Suibhne composes poetry, flies like a bird and utters prophecies: all three disciplines common to shamans world-wide. His contest with the Hag of the Mill is, like Taliesin's shape-shifting contest with Ceridwen, a way of describing a shamanic initiation. It is also reminiscent of various accounts of the struggles between rival 'sorcerers' in South American shamanism. The nickname 'Geilt' (which is applied to Suibhne) is generally taken to mean 'madman'. The Irish equivalent of the Welsh *gwylt*, meaning 'wild', it was attached to the figure of Merlin, who shares many of the shamanic attributes of Suibhne. It is more than possible that the word 'geilt' or 'gwelt' is the Celtic equivalent of the word shaman: an inspired, flighting madman who could foretell the future and who lived in close communion with animals.

These far-away tales may not seem to have much to tell us today, but studied in the proper way and in the context of world-wide shamanic practice they reveal a great deal. They also illustrate the general method by which the various techniques and methods set forth in this book were arrived at. Following hints and clues from the whole range of Celtic myth-lore, poetry and literature, it has been possible to identify much of the original Celtic shamanic practice.

It might well be asked why, in the late twentieth century, it should be considered desirable to adopt the methods and beliefs of the oldest spiritual discipline on the planet? The reasons which might be given are numerous. For instance, shamanism has informed every other spiritual discipline, and in the parts of the world where it is still practised in a more or less unbroken tradition, the messages which call out to us, in the modern Western metropolis, are as vital and urgent now as they have ever been. Celtic shamanism was, and is, a living thing. It teaches us respect for the rest of creation – a theme which, in our destructive age, is of the utmost importance – and it shows us new approaches to living: ways beyond the linear time-lines with which we bind ourselves: out of the realm in which we see without seeing, hear without hearing; touch without feeling and breathe the air without tasting or scenting the news it brings us of our world. Shamanism can teach all of this. But above all it restores a quality to our lives which many of us have missed for a long time. This is the sense of wonder, and of an ability to pass beyond this three-dimensional world into a fourth dimension: the Otherworld of which the Celts knew so much and of which they have left so eloquent a testimony.

But perhaps the best answer, in the long run, is that shamanism is a way of working with the self, with the elements from which we are all constructed, and that it thus cuts across all the self-imposed barriers of race, religion and culture. No matter what your persuasion or religious instinct, shamanism reaches beyond these to a point where all are one.

I first became aware of shamanism in the sixties when, drifting away from the drug-culture of the time, in common with many young people, I began to look for other ways to achieve 'enlightenment'. At the time Carlos Castaneda's best-selling books were beginning to appear, and were the only ones available on the market which dealt with shamanism at a popular level. Though I found them fascinating, I instinctively felt they were not for me. I knew little, then, of the doubts cast upon Castaneda's work by anthropologists working in similar areas; today I would say that they present a number of fascinating aspects of the shaman's art and that, ultimately, it is not important whether they are 'true' in the proper sense of the word. They still give a remarkably powerful impression of what it means to be a shaman.

Then I moved away from the whole question of shamanism into other disciplines – Sufism, ritual magic, wicca, and finally, Catholicism.

None of these was wholly satisfying, though each contributed some-thing to my search. Eventually I was drawn back to the old religions of Britain, and to the Celtic myths which embodied them. I experienced an intensive period of training with a group celebrating the ancient myster-ies of the year (I have written about this in *Voices from the Circle*, edited by Caitlín Matthews). But once again I moved on, becoming at this time aware of North American shamanism, discovering *Black Elk Speaks* and Frank Walters', *Book of the Hopi*, both of which I devoured. I felt a sense of recognition in the traditions of these visionary people, and sought to read more about the Amerindians and their way of life.

Finally I made it to America, and it was indeed like 'coming home'. During my stay I experienced the kind of intense dream states which happen only rarely: a vividly lucid awareness in which I met and talked with an Indian shaman who called himself simply Old Man. I had experienced this kind of inner contact before, and knew enough to tell a genuine vision from a wish-fulfilling dream.

Old Man was astonishing. His humour was like nothing I had encountered before, and he was quite ruthless in making me see the old stereotypes of my life with new eyes. Before I returned to Britain he told me that he would keep in contact, but that I must seek out my own native shamanism, despite the difficulties I would encounter.

Back home I became aware of the similarities between *all* kinds of shamanism, whether North American, Siberian, Australian, Esquimaux or whatever, and that the native myths which I had studied and worked with for over twenty years were themselves the last vestiges of Celtic shamanism. This realization, and a prolonged and intensive period of study, resulted in my two books on Taliesin, a Welsh bard of the sixth century, in whose writings I discovered the bones of the shamanic practice. I learned a new sense of awareness in this time, a closer relationship with nature, and an understanding of my place in the unthinkable vastness of Creation. Old Man kept his word and has remained with me, offering a rare vision and sometimes revealing my own tradition through his eyes.

The word 'shaman' is of Tungusc origin (*saman*) and originates in the region of the Altai mountains of Siberian Russia. It is only one of a number of words used by various cultures to denote someone who, through trance and ecstasy, enters other states of being to that in which he or she usually lives, returning with news from which all of humanity (as represented by the tribe) can benefit. The word shaman can be translated as meaning 'to burn up, to set on fire' and this refers to the ability of the shaman to work with the energy of heat. This is the same skill which enables fire-walkers to remain unhurt and yogis to sit naked in the snow for several days without dying of exposure through the expert understanding and manipulation of energies and temperatures within the body. We can also see here a reference to the feverishness of inspiration with which the shaman works: indeed, anyone who has ever suffered from a fever, whether it be simple 'flu or something more serious, already knows what it means to feel like a shaman. In the twilight place of non-being, *between* the worlds, the insights, wisdom and understanding of the shaman are born.

Other meanings of the word 'shaman' are 'one who is excited, moved, raised up'. It has also been traced to the Indo-European root word meaning 'to know', or sometimes 'to heat oneself'. Thus at base the word refers to what its most famous explorer, Mircea Eliade, refers to as 'an archaic technique of ecstasy'; a way of perceiving one's place in creation, and of finding the active role one can play in it. The emphasis is, above all, on the word *active*. Shamans are continually working on themselves: shaping, honing, planing their spiritual selves in such a way as to develop better and more lasting ways to encounter and interact with dimensions of the sacred.

A word about the general use of the word 'shaman'. In the Tungusc language the word *saman* refers to people of both sexes, and I have therefore generally adopted it as such throughout, occasionally using the word shamanka, and varying the use of the pronouns 'he' and 'she'.

But the purpose of this book is not to examine the history of shamanism, nor even its specifically Celtic aspects. It is intended to provide a series of techniques for its practice in the modern world, based upon Celtic sources, or in line with what we know of Celtic belief-systems from the earliest times. It is thus neither a source-book nor a historical–anthropological survey, but a reflection of a *living tradition* – and of the supremely practical approach to life which is the essence of shamanism.

There are twelve basic steps towards becoming a working shaman or shamanka. These, which constitute a glyph which I have termed 'The Shaman's Ladder', will be dealt with fully in Chapter 5. For the moment we may summarize them as follows:

1. *The First Realization*: An awakening to shamanic awareness.
2. *Opposition*: The difficulties encountered at the beginning of the journey.
3. *Death*: The first rite of passage in the making of a shaman.
4. *Awakening*: The discovery of individual potential.
5. *Meeting*: The first encounter with inner reality.
6. *Travelling*: Passing within and exploring the Otherworld.

7. *Totems*: Discovering and learning from the totem beasts and power animals.
8. *The Inner Shaman*: Encountering an inner guide and teacher.
9. *Spirit World*: Learning to move at will through the place of the spirits.
10. *Acceptance*: Second rite of passage and the beginning of outer work.
11. *Vision*: The ability to see into the inner realms and to divine future events.
12. *The Second Realization*: The integration of inner work into outer life.

Implicit within this larger structure are five clearly defined principles which constitute shamanic awareness. These are:

1. The discovery of your relationship to all created beings, animal, vegetable and mineral.
2. Becoming aware of the shape and dimensions of the cosmos around you.
3. Becoming conversant with alternative states of being, learning to make contact and work with the totem beasts and power animals who dwell there. (These concepts are fully explained in Chapter 4.)
4. Contacting your inner shamanic teacher, who will take you on to the next stage of your training.
5. The ability to journey into the Otherworldly realms, where you will encounter the gods and begin a more advanced stage of training.

The first four chapters of this book are designed to enable you to become fully conversant with all of these principles, and to prepare the way for the ascent of the Shaman's Ladder. Chapter 5 marks the turning point, in which you will learn to master the technique of journeying to and from the inner realms. Chapters 6 to 9 expand upon this foundation by showing how the basic shamanic principles discussed earlier can be applied to everyday life.

One of the most important legacies of both the Celtic and the Amerindian peoples is their holistic world-view, which implies no division between flesh and spirit, no inferiority between the sexes, no feeling that because they 'own' the world they can use it as they like. To most of us living in the west today, the whole of life, including its spirituality, is based on an ethic which has separated people from the rest of creation, divided spirit from flesh, mind from matter. To the shaman this was never so; he, or she, inhabited a world in which there were no such divisions. Everything was sacred, every action religious (which had a *reaction* in the inner realms). The shaman or shamanka operated as a medium between the inner and outer worlds, as well as those of spirit or flesh, *which were seen as having no separate existence.* For them, the reality of the otherworld was always accessible.

The shaman, then, is the servant of the sacred, rather than its priest. The shaman operates, as he or she has always done, as an agent of the numinous, plying his or her way between one world and the other. To understand this, which is crucial to the practice of shamanism, we must learn to see with eyes other than those we normally use, to view creation as a totality, not as something divided into realms of matter and spirit, or indeed of inner and outer. This book is thus about ways of learning to live in harmony with everything in creation: the elements, the animals which walk the land, the birds which fly in the air, the fish which swim in the seas and rivers, the myriad mineral and plant life-forms. We are all part of a single creation, and by separating ourselves off we have caused irreparable damage to ourselves and our environment.

If we begin by acknowledging this, we have taken the first step towards becoming modern shamans and shamankas. We cannot, of course, do so in exactly the same way as our ancestors did. Time has moved on; things have changed as much in the last few hundred years as in several thousand before, and we are no longer the same people. Even the most rurally situated practitioner of shamanism, though possessing a distinct advantage over his or her urban counterpart, is still more urbanized than the least skilled practitioner in the jungles of South America.

Nevertheless, I still think that we can learn a vast amount from shamanism, and that it is a mistaken belief that it can only take place in the wilds, or at an ancient site where people have worshipped for centuries. Those who live in cities know as well as anyone what it means to be born into a world to which we have done so much harm. In fact, it is almost a positive advantage to live in such a place. The effort involved in encouraging an awareness of the natural world in the concrete forests of our large cities, can help focus our energies and our intent most effectively. The harbouring of earth energies, of the few parched stretches of green we call parks, is as much a part of shamanic activity as building a circle or worshipping the old gods at an ancient site.

The true learning begins when we acknowledge our place in the scheme of things, which may be a less central one than we have believed in the past, but which is no less important for all that. This done, we have to learn to be part of the natural world again, by working with the energies present both in ourselves and around us. Once these have been brought into proper alignment, the new age eagerly anticipated by so many people will begin to dawn. By working in harmony with the natural forces which govern Creation, we may begin to see beyond the age of darkness through which we are still, perhaps unwittingly, passing.

I am very well aware that shamanism cannot be taught, especially through the written word. The best that can be done is to impart some sense of the kind of world the shaman inhabits, which is just as relevant to contemporary human beings as to the people of the past. It is my hope that by following the exercises and meditations contained herein this world will become more accessible to the prospective shaman or shamanka. From that point the real work begins, inner training commences, and the journey to the furthest extent of the universe can be undertaken. Ideally this book should be regarded as a jumping-off point, a spring-board to the infinite, where the newly fledged shaman or shamanka will learn to fly in earnest.

It should also be understood that reading this book and practising some or all of its teachings will not automatically make you a shaman. It will almost certainly improve the quality of your life, though the process includes a radical breaking down of the structures with which we surround ourselves, which is often painful and far from easy. You must be prepared to work very hard indeed, and to embrace the general 'philosophy' of shamanism, that everything has life and is part of a sacred whole. After this, a minimum of two years' work with an inner teacher is required. Even then you may not attain an experience of the inner worlds, which is a necessary adjunct to these teachings. However, if you persevere and practise hard you will, in time, find yourself transformed.

Finally it should be noted that two aspects of the shaman's life overlap: the exploration of inner, non-physical realms, and the practice of the healer's art. In this book I shall deal primarily with the former. This is not to say that the ability to heal is not important, but it requires a more specialized discipline and cannot be learned from the pages of a book. Nor can one begin any shamanic work until one has travelled in the inner realms and learned to become familiar with the dimensions of the otherworld. Therefore, while some examples of simpler healing methods will be described (see Chapter 7), more advanced techniques, requiring formal training, should not be attempted until the practitioner has been working shamanically for *at least a year*. Another kind of healing – that of the earth – will be dealt with at greater length and in more detail. And since in healing our mother the earth we also heal ourselves, a lesson of great importance will be learned along the way.

Writing this book has been in the nature of a personal visionary journey. I have learned much about my own tradition in the process and look forward to continuing my explorations of the inner worlds. It is also my foremost desire to strike up a continuing dialogue with those other cultures which possess a largely unbroken shamanic tradition, to show how they harmonize, and to bring them closer together. It is my hope that one day we may see again a universal network of shamanism, which will embody some of the same benefits and blessings it once brought to a younger, less tired, less soul-sick world.

John Matthews

NOTE TO THE READER

This book constitutes an exploration of ancient shamanic techniques normally undertaken with a qualified teacher. The reader is therefore solely responsible for his or her own action in undertaking the training offered herein. It should also be clearly understood that the methods and techniques described in this book are not a substitute for either psychological or medical treatment.

Part 1

THEORY

1 Recovering Your Senses

'The power of solitude is great
and beyond understanding.'

A. Rasmussen

THE SHAMAN'S VISION

IN THE WEST WE HAVE BEEN TAUGHT to believe we are corrupt and fallen beings, separated from the spiritual realms, the natural state of Paradise and grace. This is so entrenched that even those professing no religious belief are deeply influenced by it. The way of the shaman, on the other hand, is based on a fundamental understanding that people are an integral part of the natural world, which is neither corrupt nor fallen. We are in continuous contact with the spiritual realms quite simply because they are all around us, and we are part of them.

The Western passion for material wealth is more damaging than we realize. The tribal peoples of North or South America, or the Aborigines of Australia, enjoy a far richer life than we can ever hope to possess. They live under a continuous spiritual tradition which has never strayed from the premise that they are part of creation. The Celts, too, understood this; it formed the basis of their traditions and rituals. In trying to recover the way of the Celtic shamans we must come to terms with this way of seeing and feeling, and must abandon much of what we know as a 'normal' way of life in the late twentieth century.

This is not, of course, intended as an outright denigration, or rejection, of modern technocentric culture and civilization for the sake of it. We have discovered many good things, many benefits which should be preserved. What I am proposing is not that we should discard all we have learned, but that we should try to regain the freshness and inner power of the shaman's vision. Once we grasp the essential understanding that everything is part of us, as we are a part of it, and that it is not necessary to believe in a linear progression from 'A' at birth to 'Z' at death, having accomplished (for which read 'acquired') as much as possible on the way; once we begin to see life as a spiral rather than a straight line, we have achieved one of the fundamentals of the shaman's way. From here we can begin to explore the true realm in which we live, follow the network of radiating lines from a central point (at best ourselves, or at least where we stand in relation to the universe) into the deepest (or highest) planes of the spirit.

We have taught ourselves to believe we are alone in a hostile world. Instead we should begin to see that we are co-workers with Nature, that we are interdependent with and upon it. We must realize that we are its defenders, not its enemies; its caretakers, who look after it so that it can continue to provide for us.

The shamans see all of this because they have learned to travel within the natural world, which is also the realm of the spirits, of the animal helpers they are able to summon in times of need. This understanding makes them unique, but we are all capable of attaining this state if we really want to. We have to re-learn much that we have forgotten, but the heritage that is ours for the asking has always been there; we simply have to learn how to explore it. We must reject our current materialistic society, and remind ourselves of the values of a less complicated age, simpler not in its structures and methodologies, which are every bit as complex as our own, but in its regard for nature, time and goals. If we can achieve this at both a personal and world-wide level, we will have taken a step of such importance that nothing will ever be quite the same again.

Anthropologist Joseph Epes Brown, in his essay on 'The Roots of Renewal', notes that the current desire to 'conquer' space is a reflection of our desire to find a further extension of our self-imposed reality. He goes on: 'The quest is futile of course, especially embarked upon to satisfy ultimate concerns, since even such seemingly limitless reaches of space, being always of a material and thus quantitive order, are still within the domain of limitation. (*Seeing With A Native Eye*')

Outside this self-limiting domain we can see things not only more clearly but also in context. Problems, whether personal or global, appear in a different light when seen against a background of spiritual reality, unhindered by petty concerns of materialism, and which exists outside the artificial boundaries of time and space. Shamanism is experienced with the blood and fibre of the body; it is not informed by the intellect alone. If you understand this much, this book should be no more than a beginning for your own journey. Remember that the watchword is 'wonder'; everything is filled with wonder, though nothing is superior – simply marvel at the experience of communicating with a world that is bursting with created abundance. With this in mind you have already entered the shamanic universe; the teachings and signposts that follow will help you develop this awareness. Go swiftly and gently, and your path will surely be filled with wonder.

EXPECTATIONS AND REALIZATIONS

The apparent ease with which you can assume a shamanic state through the practices outlined here should not cause you to undervalue the experience. It is the long-term effect of the experience, what you choose to 'do' with it, that matters. Above all it is important that you learn to *live* your shamanism all the time; you cannot shut it up in a box labelled 'Celtic shamanism' and set it next to similar containers marked (for example) Druidism, Hinduism, Sufism, etc. Indeed, there are shamanic aspects to all of these religions, just as there are to Christianity, Islam, and Judaism. Celtic shamanism seeks to enter deeply into the world of the ancient races of the British Isles, but it does *not* seek to imitate or emulate every aspect of Celtic life and attitudes. It takes what may be considered the most appropriate things for our time, and attempts to integrate them into everyday living.

   These ideas and teachings will be of little use if you do not *believe* in yourself as a shaman. Many of the skills you will learn to work with come from within, but a great deal comes from without, from what is generally referred to as 'the spirit realm'. When the inner power of the shaman rises to meet the descending power of the spiritual realms, there occurs a spark of energy which transforms the man or woman sitting in his or her sacred circle. It gives them the necessary strength and understanding to journey inwards to the centre of themselves – a centre which is nowhere and yet everywhere, and which exists on more than one plane. This experience is so astonishing, so marvellous in its complexity and richness, that those who feel it are at once empowered by it forever.

   However, there are other emotions which you must learn to come to terms with. Among these are loneliness, compassion, love, fear, ecstasy and joy, each of which you will encounter in one form or another through the practice of shamanism. Disciplines such as concentration, the abandonment of will, and the search for happiness (a word which has been much devalued in our time, but which still best describes the balanced state resulting from an acceptance of our place in the scheme of things), will need to be mastered as well.

You will find a number of exercises and techniques thoughout this book. These are designed to help you realize your shamanic capacity without the need of a personal teacher (this role will be assumed at a later stage by an inner teacher, see Chapter 4). You should approach these instructions with an open mind and receptive spirit. The mind has a way of killing the intuitive and the spontaneous, and throughout your shamanic work these attributes are vital starting-points.

You will be required to do a certain amount of meditation and visualization, and this is a good time to mention the basic techniques involved. If you are already used to these practices you need not read this; if not, it is important to realize at this stage that meditation involves switching off your everyday consciousness as far as possible, and tuning into your feeling, intuitive self. You may not have had much experience of this before, and it may take a while to adjust. If you find that the exercises are not working properly for you, keep trying. It is important not to give up since practice is the best way of learning, and habit educates the intuitive senses better than most things.

When you meditate you should sit in a quiet place where you will not be disturbed. Choose an upright chair (to avoid falling asleep) and sit straight, with hands on knees and feet flat on the floor. (Avoid crossing your legs as this can become uncomfortable after a while, and impedes the flow of energy through your body.) Relax and breathe deeply to a regular count. I personally breathe in to a count of two, hold for a count of one, breathe out to a count of two, but you may wish to experiment with this until you find the rhythm which suits you best. (An alternative method, involving various postures, is discussed in Chapter 5.)

Gradually clear your mind of everyday thoughts, worries, fears. This is not as easy as it sounds. We are submitted to so much outside stimuli from radios, television, aircraft, cars and so on, that we are cursed with 'butterfly mentality', and find it hard to concentrate on anything for more than a second. Most people complain of mind-wandering when they first start meditating: a hundred-and-one small thoughts come tumbling into our minds as soon as we are still and quiet. With time and a little patience these factors can be filtered out, and once you are truly at rest you can begin meditating on a seed-thought (a word or phrase, or question to which you require an answer). Alternatively, if you are called upon to visualize, once your mind is still you can begin to allow the images described (which you might like to read onto a tape and play back while visualizing) to rise in your consciousness. Try to 'be there', to enter the scenes described, as fully as possible. The more solid the images become, the more satisfying the experience will be.

This allows the changes in consciousness, which are part of becoming a shaman, to take place naturally. From the still point within you will be able to journey forth in search of other dimensions. In Celtic terms this is known as 'entering the Otherworld'; essentially you are entering a trancelike state. Other techniques for this include various bodily postures (discussed in Chapter 5) and the use of a drum to induce a change in consciousness.

None of these techniques is harmful. Falling into a trance state is simply another way of saying that you are entering a space *within you*, in which you are able to filter out the concerns of your everyday consciousness and become aware of other states of being. These are sometimes referred to as altered states of consciousness, or as religious ecstasy, during which the individual becomes *conscious of a greater dimension of reality*. All shamans work from this basis, and you will need to become familiar with it before you can successfully approach your training.

The experience of a trance state varies, not only among individuals, but also from one occasion to another. Sometimes you may feel an unusual degree of heat, or of cold; you may find yourself shaking, or becoming aware of either a brilliant light around you or an intense area of darkness. These are physiological reactions to spiritual conditions. They are akin to the varied emotions which can be evoked by looking at great art or listening to music. Some will bring tears to the eyes. Others will uplift or inspire.

Most people who experience trance-states agree that they are accompanied by a feeling of great well-being. No matter what the exact nature of the experience may be, this response is almost always recognizable, and is the product of an increased awareness of being at one with Creation. Sometimes you may see yourself, or others, in a startlingly different way. We may think here of the Round Table knights, who saw the Grail and were suddenly able to perceive one another in a wholly new way.

The trance-state is thus about breaking out of old and outworn patterns of awareness. The shamans know of many worlds and many levels of being in which they are able to travel. They experience the wonder of Creation every time they journey by this means into other dimensions.

At the end of any session of meditation or visualization (which should be no more than twenty minutes to begin with) always earth yourself by drinking and eating immediately, or by doing some mundane task. You will also find it useful to keep a note-book or diary of your realizations, since these will often have a bearing on your later work and will sometimes become clearer and more meaningful with the passage of time.

With this information you should be able to proceed with any of the exercises contained in this book. Other, more specific, techniques, will be dealt with where this becomes necessary.

One of the first things you must do is to learn to face your self-imposed limitations, your fears and self-deceptions. We all suffer from these, whether we acknowledge them or not, and as a shaman you will learn, in time, to be free of such things. This is *all* that is holding you back from realizing your shamanic self.

It is equally important to understand the need for periods of solitude in which you must come to terms with your emotions. You may proceed some considerable way along the path without realizing this, and it can be extremely painful, but once you have learned to know and understand your true self, your whole approach to living will be changed beyond recognition. You will no longer feel inadequate or self-denying; your strength of will will grow and continue to develop. You need never again say that you 'hate yourself' (a state of mind shared by far more people than you may realize). So, take some time to be alone; if possible go into the countryside and stay near one of the less-frequented ancient sites which possess a sacred dimension. Even here it may be difficult to be totally alone: this is one of the problems of the modern world and must be dealt with as best you can. In effect the kind of solitude necessary for the shaman is an inner 'aloneness'. Only by this means will you learn that to lose everything is to gain everything; only thus will you be able to recognize the many facets of your inner self, and to separate the true from the false.

Here is a path to help this process to occur in a natural way.

The Cave of Care

Imagine yourself in a great cave, its roof a huge arch above you, its walls stretching out on either side and vanishing into darkness. When you feel that the cave is sufficiently solid and real to you, visualize a circle of light around you. This is for your personal protection and ensures that no matter what occurs next no harm can come to you. When you are completely sure of your security, begin to consider your greatest fear. Try, if you can, to give it form and shape. Then, when you are ready, call it into the cave and face it. Do the same with your limiting and self-deceiving selves, and also with your ideal self. Subject them all to careful scrutiny. Some will appear glamorous, some the reverse, but which is the better? Some fears are so deep-seated that you may not recognize them as such. Take time to consider the things that most upset you; an emotional signpost may denote more than one kind of inner response. See these forms for what they are: shadows of your real self. Then, begin to make careful changes to the images you have formed. Watch them alter before your eyes into something different. This resculpting process may take many forms. Your fearful self may look shimmery and insubstantial: shape it to become confident and firm; your illusory self may appear suspicious or beglamoured: give it some hard reality by seeing it perform a mundane piece of work, such as gardening, or washing-up. Remember what you see and feel, and try to bring back a sense of your restored inner self from the meditation.

(If you prefer you can substitute a forest clearing for the cave; in either case the results will be the same.)

This is not an easy path to tread, and it may need to be travelled several times before the desired result is achieved. However, its importance cannot be over-estimated. Before any shaman accepts new pupils he will subject them to rigorous tests and trials of this kind. The effect of these is to dismantle some of the old and outworn concepts which lie within every person, and to rebuild upon strong foundations. There is no point in taking up the practice of shamanism if you are weak and unprepared. So take your time with this exercise, which may be less tempting than some of the later ones, but which is of paramount importance since it helps form the foundation on which you can then build.

At first, you will probably experience some confusion, and there are bound to be painful realizations. You should seriously question your reason for wanting to be a shaman at this point. The answer may be quite different from what you expect, as may the shadow-selves you perceive in the cave or forest. Later you will be able to call upon the help of inner guides and helpers, but it is essential that, in the initial stage of your training, you face certain things alone.

THE PROBLEM OF POWER

Something you will need to come to terms with is power. As a shaman or shamanka you will learn to deal with powerful beings, as well as learning to find and release your personal power. You may already feel that you have your own power, or you may feel disempowered. This depends upon the circumstances of your life, and gives an idea of whether or not you are in line with your destiny. You may be in a situation at home or work which is disagreeable to you in some way.

You should always try to deal with such problems at an early stage in your shamanic training; to learn to take charge and initiate yourself into your true inner strength.

Just as the Cave of Care meditation taught you to face your fears, so the one which follows is designed to help you to acknowledge your inner power and to begin the reshaping of your life.

The Shape of Being

In this meditation you find yourself back in the cave/forest where you faced your worst fears. Now you feel more confident of yourself and your abilities, but you still have to ask the question: 'What is the shape of my life, and what do I need to do to ensure that it follows the shape laid down for me?' (This does not mean that you have no freedom of choice; simply that a pattern exists which you may or may not choose to follow, but which is nonetheless offered to you.)

Within the cave/clearing all is still. You enter a state of peace and harmony with yourself; all the cares and fears of your life in the mundane world fall away. Eventually you reach a point which enables you to view your life objectively.

Now you see a number of stones scattered about the floor of the cave or clearing, on each of which is a symbol relating in some way to your home, work, partnerships, friends, enemies, hopes and desires – all the elements which form the pattern of your life.

Begin collecting the stones, and consider what these building-blocks mean to you. How do you view your relationships, your work, your children if you have any? What would you change if you could? What are your dreams and ambitions; how many have you implemented so far? Consider each stone. Weigh it in either hand, feel if it balances or whether it seems to want to roll away or turn over . . .

Now, taking your time, begin to set the stones into a pattern which pleases you. This may sound easy, but you will find that you spend a lot of time moving the stones from place to place until you establish the right relationships. Pay particular attention to which ones are easy to position – foundations, perhaps? Which are central to the pattern? Which are peripheral?. . .

When you have finished (allow yourself a reasonable amount of time) study the pattern until you are thoroughly familiar with it. Take note of the way certain stones relate to each other, the way some seem less important than others. Then, slowly and carefully, return to ordinary consciousness and draw the pattern in a notebook, putting in the symbols as you remember them, or what they represent in words.

Keep this and study it again in a few weeks; if necessary repeat the meditation and observe how it has changed. Whether or not you follow the pattern you have made, you have made an important step towards understanding the shape of your life. You have also learned a great deal about power. In the meditation you could choose where to put the stones, and how to order them into a pleasing pattern. This took a certain kind of inner strength, although you may not feel that you possess the same control over events in your outer life. The truth is that power, as with so many other things, is relative. You may well be using more energy than you need in certain areas of your life; less in others. This has to do with balance and, as a practising shaman, you have to come to terms with this.

Throughout this book you will learn ways to address such problems, to bring yourself into proper alignment with the cosmos around you in its manifest and unmanifest forms. But, at every level, you will encounter the need for power, and for its right use. It is at this point, before your real training begins, that you need to consider your relationship to the power that is awakening within you. You must understand that power is, of itself, neither good nor bad; the uses to which it is put decide this. How you choose to interpret this is very largely up to you, but the cost, in terms of spiritual currency, is always high. It is important, for example, not to look on the power you hold as a personal possession, and thereby to appropriate it. You should also realize that if the beings, experiences, and knowledge which you acquire in the Otherworld are inapplicable to this world, it is inappropriate for you to use them at all.

There are no simple ways of dealing with this; experience alone will tell you the best way to go about it. You will soon know: your totem beast or power animal will tell you if your inner teacher does not (see Chapters 3 and 4). But always remember that you are responsible for what you do with your shamanic abilities. This should not to be taken lightly; if you do, you are likely to be the first to suffer the effects of misused power, which has a tendency to blow back in the faces of those who forget that they are part of a greater whole, and that the power entrusted to them is their responsibility to use in the right way.

In effect the shaman must constantly review the way he or she uses such power, to be sure that it is only for the good of others. There is even some doubt as to whether you should use such power for yourself at all. The answer rests in the question of what *kind* of use you make of it. The use of power for self-aggrandisement or personal gain is certainly wrong; using it to help yourself find balance, or to restore your health, is within the bounds of shamanic practice, since you must be allowed to make of your abilities the best that you can. Ultimately the decision on such matters rests mainly with the individual.

MOVING IN MANY WORLDS

The shaman has access to an immense number of worlds. We all possess ways of entering these, but have forgotten how to find them. The shaman has not forgotten; he or she uses the windows of the senses, and a communion with the natural world, to enter and live for a time within these other states of being. The rituals, ceremonies and meditations in this book are aimed at teaching you how to let go of your normal way of life so that you can 'remember' these Otherworldly teachings and reach them. There is a great store of knowledge which has always been available, but which we have forgotten how to access, because of the way we live.

Essentially, in all shamanic practice, you are in a one-to-one situation, either with your teacher (inner or outer) or with the gods you have chosen to work with (or who have chosen you). In Celtic mythology stories abound of heroes who had this singular relationship with deity. Thus Taliesin and Ceridwen, Cuchulainn and the Morrigan, Fionn and Sabha, and so on. These people, faerie men and women, gods, Other-worldly kings and queens, invariably set seemingly impossible tasks and then help either in person or through intermediaries. This agrees with shamanic practice, where the shaman consistently calls upon Other-world beings for help. In Siberian practice these become specifically 'spirit helpers'; their Celtic equivalents are the people of the Otherworld. By working with these tremendous inner forces, you are seeking, finally, to engage your higher self, to wake up your sleeping senses and re-establish contact with the natural world – a contact which was, at one time, taken for granted.

It is said that shamans sometimes 'steal' their power by trickery, and there are many instances of this in Celtic lore. In a variant version of the Taliesin story, young Gwion Bach presents himself as possessing the secret of fire to the three wise women (gwyddans) who guard the Cauldron of Inspiration. Then, while they are away, he steals the wisdom of the cauldron. In another story Cuchulainn, the Ultonian hero, attempts to catch the Salmon of Wisdom from the Well of Sagais. He is prevented by a diminutive character named Senbecc ua Ebric (The Little Old One) who after trying, unsuccessfully, to persuade Cuchulainn to give up the salmon he has caught, sings him to sleep and takes the fish for himself.

These stories show that the shamans sometimes have to trick themselves into accessing their own power and wisdom. That we, in our own very un-shamanic times, must do the same, will become increasingly obvious as we proceed.

Sharpening your senses

We use our senses all the time: we feel, see, hear, smell, taste and touch. But in reality they only tell us a little of what we could experience. If we live shamanically we will learn to hear words that others cannot, to smell the scents of the Otherworld, to taste the pure waters of the Well of Dreams, to touch into our selves more deeply than ever before.

Learning how to 'see' is one of the primary shamanic functions. In the West we are conditioned from birth to see what we have been told is there: the 'real' world which can be perceived by the five senses. Shamans are not taught in this way; they seek to free themselves of such conditioning, to see and feel with their *inner* senses. For them there are seven senses, not five, as Taliesin well knows:

'One is for instinct,
two is for feeling,
three is for speaking,
four is for tasting,
five is for seeing,
six is for hearing,
seven is for smelling . . .

Thus you must learn to do the same. Once you have succeeded you will become aware of a wholly different kind of reality, the Otherworld, so movingly portrayed in this quotation from *The Voyage of Bran mac Febal to the Land of Women*:

The size of the plain, the number of the host,
Colours glisten with pure glory,
A fair stream of silver, cloths of gold,
Afford a welcome with abundance.

A beautiful game, most delightful,
They play (sitting) at the luxurious wine,
Men and gentle women under a bush
Without sin, without crime . . .

A wood with blossom and fruit,
On which is the vine's veritable fragrance,
A wood without decay, without defect,
On which are leaves of golden hue.

(Trans. by Kuno Meyer)

Once you become aware of the existence of such alternative states of being, you will find this beautiful place, and all the dimensions of creation, opening up around you more and more fully.

There are many ways of tricking your consciousness to see beyond the manifest world. You do so every time you read an absorbing book, during which time you enter an alternative frame of reality which is just as vivid to you as anything else. Sometimes this can linger, for a few moments, after you put the book down. If you work hard you can begin to extend those few moments into hours, and then whole days, weeks, months and years. This is not, of course, to suggest that you enter a realm of fantasy in which you lose contact with the mundane world; simply that you should train yourself to be aware of other possibilities, alternative realities which exist *alongside* the daily round of being.

One of the most common ways of accomplishing this is to enter an altered state of being in which neither time nor space, nor indeed reality as we have been taught to view it, has any existence. The best known method is the form of meditation called visualization, which we utilized to visit the Cave of Care. This kind of meditation is really a matter of placing oneself into a passive state and then allowing a series of directed images to rise in the mind. Initially it is difficult for most untrained Westerners to concentrate on anything for more than a moment at a time. The constant stream of outer stimuli to which we are subjected for most of our waking lives has given us grasshopper-consciousness. We have to learn to rid ourselves of that and to concentrate our entire being into what the old Christian mystics called 'one-pointedness'. There are many ways to do this, but the most tried and trusted method is still to sit, for a varied length of time *every day*, in a quiet place and with a specific intent. Gradually the duration can be extended and the complexity of the meditation increased.

To work at all in this way requires a good deal of concentration and self-discipline. You may need to sit, very still, for as long as an hour at a time before you feel anything. This is a great deal harder than you may think. Firstly you will certainly suffer from 'mind-wandering', a well-attested problem which faces all who come to meditation for the first time. Our butterfly minds will drift off rather than settle to a period of quiet, and it requires some skill – not to mention trickery! – to persuade the mind to 'switch off' for long enough for us to attain a different mode of being. I personally found this really difficult when I first began to work shamanically; it took months of effort to bring my mind sufficiently under control to be able to meditate on chosen themes. So, do not despair if you have difficulty with any of the exercises in this book which require concentration. Keep trying, stubbornly, until your mind gets used to the idea.

What follows is a visualization which draws specifically upon the Celtic tradition. It takes you into the Otherworld and permits you to see how it functions. And, along the way, you may learn something new about yourself. The ancient Celtic shamans would have prepared themselves for days before undertaking such a journey; the visualization enables you to omit these procedures (of which you will learn more later). For the time being the most practical way to experience the visualization is to read the text aloud into a tape-recorder (or get a friend to do so) then, with eyes closed, and sitting comfortably on a straight-backed chair (to prevent falling asleep), breathe deeply and steadily for a while until you have stilled the furious pace of daily time and space. Then switch on the tape and listen. Try hard to 'be there' in the scenes described, and take note afterwards of any significant realizations which come to you. You may not fully understand all that occurs at this stage, nor be necessarily conversant with the figures you encounter (if you wish you can look them up in Chapter 4, but it sometimes ensures a more powerful initial response if you are not familiar with such details).

Caer Arianrhod

Let yourself sink deeply into meditation. Breathe deeply and regularly and as you do so allow your consciousness of the room around you to fade into a distant background. Now imagine that you are standing on top of a green mound. It is twilight and the sun is setting behind you, casting your shadow long upon the ground. Over your head the great arch of the heavens stretches, darkening to deepest blue and already pricked out by the first faint shimmering of stars.

Below you on the flat green plain which surrounds the mound you see a figure moving, coming nearer. He begins to ascend the mound, climbing swiftly on his long legs. As he approaches you see that he is tall and thin, with dark hair worn long and bound about his brows with a circlet of bronze. He is dressed in dark green and carries at his back a leather bag from which he now takes a small, intricately carved harp.

He bows before you. 'I am Taliesin, Primary Chief Bard of the Island of Britain and Guardian of the Summer Stars. I am come to conduct you on a journey to the Court of Arianrhod, there to seek a vision of that which is to be. Hearken now to my words and follow where I lead.'

He begins to play upon the harp, striking chords and small flourishes of notes from the small instrument, which yet produces a sound far greater, a sound which enters into you so deeply that you lose all track of time and place and are not at all surprised to find that a silvery stairway has risen before you, leading upwards into the star-strewn sky. Like a shepherd with his sheep, Taliesin guides you onto the stairs and you begin to climb, the bard following behind, still playing the deep and magical music which holds you enthralled.

Far you climb and still further, until the earth is way below, and the immensity of the night sky extends on all sides. And now ahead you begin to see a great silvery light which you soon realize is coming from a doorway opening in the sky. The stair on which you stand leads directly to this door and you enter and find yourself at the entrance to a vast hall. The walls and roof, distant though they are, seem to be made of light, golden and silvery and shimmering. And you see that the same light now shines from the brow of Taliesin, whom you remember is also called 'the Radiant Brow'. And though he has ceased to play upon his harp, yet the music continues, greater and richer and more beautiful than before, as though his playing was but a dim echo of the true music you now hear.

Silently the bard directs you to go forward, and you walk upon a floor that seems all of gold and yet somehow translucent, filled with swirling shapes too marvellous to interpret, yet filling you with joy.

And indeed from the moment you entered this wondrous place, you have been filled with great buoyancy, well-being and clarity. All your senses feel sharper than ever before – you see, hear, smell, touch and taste everything more intensely than previously, for there is a sweet savour about the place and a gentle breeze touches your face and the music seems like a golden light within you.

Ahead you begin to see the furthest end of the hall, and it seems that the light of the place originates from there. Yet strong as it is, it is also gentle, and you are able to look without fear of being dazzled.

At the end of the hall is a vast mirror, how great you cannot say, it is set in a silver frame, the sides of which are cast in the shape of huge and ancient trees. At its top cluster seven brilliant points of light, emitting rays which form the shape of a crown.

'Behold the Crown of Arianrhod in the Court of Stars.'

Taliesin's voice rings out in the great hall and the seven starry lights seem to grow brighter as he speaks. Then, as you watch, the mirror begins to grow opaque; you no longer see yourself reflected in its depths but instead a new shape begins to form there – a figure that seems garbed in light and from whom radiance streams. The figure appears as a woman of such beauty and delicacy that she seems almost transparent: light shines from her and through her and her face is as perfect as a crystal rose. Again, you hear Taliesin:

'Behold the Queen of Stars – Arianrhod, the Silver Wheel.'

A voice speaks to you, in words that you hear not with your ears but in your mind. It is a voice as clear and bright as crystal, neither harsh nor gentle, neither loving nor unloving, the voice of one so far removed from our world that it can know nothing of our being.

'You are come to seek that which is to be.'

Until this moment you perhaps knew of no reason for coming to this place, nor of any need beyond that of your everyday life. Yet as these words, conveyed directly to your innermost self, enter your thoughts, you at once know, with absolute certainty, that this is indeed your true purpose for coming.

Though no question has been asked you answer at once in affirmation that is whole-hearted, and you are answered in turn, not with words or even sensations, but by a burgeoning and shimmering within the presence of the shining figure which you somehow perceive as approbation.

'Then behold that which you seek!'

Again the words are experienced rather than heard and you marvel as the mirror changes once again, the figure fading to allow a new form to shape itself therein. No words can convey what is revealed − only within you is the form truly revealed. Beyond personal need, it is rather the desire of all creation, given form by your wish and your need. . .

PAUSE.

At length that which you thought unknowable has gone, and with it the figure of the lady. The mirror is clear again and you see your reflection with that of the bard Taliesin, who looks at you with his bright glance, seeing the reflection of your aspiration, where it still flickers, dimmer now, but still a flame in your innermost being.

At last he bows his head, and turning about leads you back through the great hall and through the door and down the silvery stair, towards the top of the green mound, shimmering far below you.

There the bard bids you farewell, and taking out his harp once more, begins to play. And as the music surrounds you and enters you, the mound and the player begin to fade, until there is only the music left in your consciousness. You can still hear it faintly as you return to normal waking consciousness.

This is a small beginning. For a certain time − and for how long, exactly, were you away? − you have inhabited another reality, another dimension which has its own rules and where certain realizations were experienced which derived only partly from the outer world. And you have stood for a time in the presence of the Great Ones who, if you allow them, will have a vast influence on your life. You will learn more of this kind of inner journey in Chapter 5. For the moment you have taken an important step on the shaman's path: time and space are what we make them, and in the Otherworld they have another kind of reality.

SACRED TIME, SACRED SPACE

One of the first qualities which define the shamanic viewpoint is the acquisition of non-linear thought. Just as it is difficult to live in the world without time, it is even harder to break the lifetime patterns which govern our way of thinking. We are used to seeing life as a simple journey from birth to death, with a number of clearly defined points along it: school, job, marriage, home-building, children, retirement and so forth. What we need to do is to view life as a mythic spiral which passes simultaneously upwards and downwards (see Fig 1): an eternally occurring and re-occurring spiral, in which any part may touch any

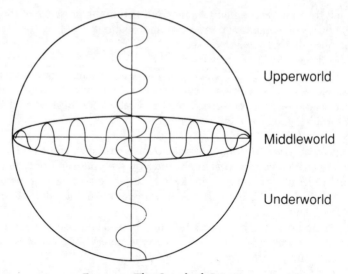

Upperworld

Middleworld

Underworld

Figure 1. The Spiral of Creation

other at the same time. In this way all eventualities become possibilities, and your own place in the pattern of things becomes ever more clearly defined.

This way of thought was germane to the ancient peoples of the world, including the Celts. To them all time was sacred, and in sacred time events occurred which affected the whole of creation. As the anthropologist Joseph Epes Brown, puts it: 'Events or processes transmitted through oral tradition tend not to be recounted in terms of time past or time future in a lineal sense. Indeed most native languages have no such terms to express this. They speak rather of a perennial reality of now.' *(Highwater: Primal Mind.)*

This in turn leads to another stage of shamanic awareness: the mastery of time itself. We live in a world governed by time. We get up, live our days and go to bed all by the ticking away of clocks, which also empty out our lives and divide them into convenient segments. Yet in reality time does not exist; it is merely a convenient way of splitting up the continuity of the days, of offering a set of convenient demarcation points on our life-journey. With it we gauge the distance we have come and still have to travel.

None of this is necessary. Learning to live without time – literally 'outside' time – is to discover one of the primary secrets of shamanism: how to live forever in a single moment and how to travel back and forth through time without need for a Wellsian time-machine.

What we are in fact seeking are sacred space and sacred time, where the mythic realities of the ancient past still exist, and are relevant to us today. In these old stories there is no neat division of time and space into comfortable blocks. Everything happens at once, and is seldom predictable.

At present, even if we become aware of the importance of myth in our lives, we tend to think of it in terms of something that happened – if indeed it happened at all – in the distant past. But *these mythic events are still happening*, and will continue to occur as long as there are those who acknowledge the power of these archetypal stories.

Study any of the old Celtic stories and you will see that references to time are virtually non-existent. At most you will find mention of seasons, day and night, the characters growing from childhood to man or womanhood and old age. This is in part because those who told them, long before they were written down, lived outside time, in an Otherworld reality. (Incidentally, this is why when you meditate you sometimes meet characters from 'history' who speak to you of the present or future – these terms are relative and have no real meaning within your visionary experience – they are not 'ghosts', but are part of the living continuity of time and space which cannot be measured with clock or ruler, but which has dimensionality of a different kind.)

To get a feel of this try writing your own mythic narrative without once referring to the modern concept of time. Consider how you might begin: 'Once upon a time. . .' What does this mean? What is the time in question, and how does it differ from the general ontological understanding of the word? Will your story have a beginning, middle and end, as good short-story writers have been told time out of mind? Or will it happen in no-time, like a dream? To the Australian Aborigines all events take place in the Dreamtime, a frame of reference which includes everything: time, space, and even so-called temporal reality itself.

Thus, when the great Celtic bard Taliesin wrote, concerning his origins:

> I was with my king
> In the heavens
> When Lucifer fell
> Into deepest hell . . .
> I was in the ark
> With Noah and Alpha.
> I witnessed the destruction
> Of Sodom and Gomorrah . . .

He meant not that he had been physically present at these events, but that his understanding of time was different from ours; that *by doing away with time he was able to be simultaneously present at all points within the continuum.*

This may seem difficult and obscure, but there are ways in which you can experience it. Try going for a long walk in the country without wearing a watch. Observe the rise and descent of the sun and try to gauge the time of day. This is the first step towards abandoning time altogether. At home, leave off your watch for a day, hide the clocks, turn off the radio and TV (always a good beginning to any shamanic practice!). After a while, during which you will look at your wrist or the clock about every two minutes, you will find that you begin to free-run. If you were able to keep this up for more than a day you would begin to fall into a natural rhythm, and when you meditated your travelling would be far deeper (outside time there is no sense of leaving or returning; you are simply suspended in the cauldron of remembrance and forgetting until you wish to return). Once you have done this, even though you may have to continue living by the clock, you will never feel quite the same about time again, but will continue to see it as relative, and a less restrictive influence on your life.

Now try meditating on the concept of time. You will quickly find that you are reduced either to linear concepts: 'Time is a continuum . . .', or to recurring cycles: 'Beginnings and endings have no beginnings or ends . . .' (Use these, or words of your own as seed-thoughts, and follow the instructions on meditation on pp18–20.) Time itself is thus shown to be illusory. But as you meditate, if you can succeed in gradually freeing yourself of words and of the thought-processes which dictate your every waking moment (whether you admit it or not) you will begin to approach the mind-set of the shaman. It may well be impossible to live in the modern world and abandon time, but once you are aware of the alternatives you are at least halfway towards freeing yourself from the regime of the clock and the calendar and of putting something infinitely more profound in its place.

Thus you have begun your great journey. You have many miles to travel; many worlds to explore; many beings to meet. All are part of the great cosmos which the Shaper-of-All made for us, to inhabit and to discover with each new day. Now that you have begun to learn what your senses can teach you, it is time to go on to the next stage of training, to learn for yourself the dimensions of the inner worlds you will soon be entering.

2 Orienteering

Coursed be the fruitful sea,
Fruitful the ranked highland,
Ranked the showery wood,
Showery the river of cataracts,
Of cataracts the lake of pools,
Of pools the hill of a well . . .

Labor Gabhala

WORKING IN MANY WORLDS

INNER ORIENTATION BEGINS WITHIN YOU and extends, first of all, into the world in which you live. In time you will learn to travel beyond the confines of your everyday consciousness, but there is no point in doing so until you have set in motion your inner compass. If you begin to feel the world around you – in front and behind, to left and right, above and below – you will start to sense your own orientation. Do you, for example, walk with your head inclined towards the earth, or tilted to look at the sky? Are you left- or right-handed, or ambidextrous? Are you only capable of seeing in a forward direction, with your eyes, or can you sense things behind or to either side? When you have answered these questions you have begun to understand the compass that works within you; with it, as you study the various methods outlined here, you will begin to be aware of dimensions other than the one in which you generally move.

The importance of these journeys to inner worlds cannot be over-emphasized. They are the means by which you establish a true under-standing of the cosmos. When you enter the Otherworld, you perceive not only that dimension, but also the manifest world in a totally new way. We learn to see ourselves clearly, to abandon the state of self-imposed exile in which we live for most of our waking lives. It is in the inner realms that we derive our spiritual empowerment, which enables us to enter the limitless dimensions of inner space.

The Celts had a deep and abiding awareness of the inner worlds. Here are some brief descriptions, taken from various sources, which give some idea of the marvellous richness of the Celtic Otherworld. The first is from the writings of an eighteenth-century Irish bard, Michael Comyn; the second from a medieval story about the great Ultonian hero Cuchulainn; and the third is from the writings of Taliesin, the sixth-century Welsh bard whose work contains so many clues to the practice of Celtic shamanism.

Abundant there are honey and wine,
and ought else the eye has beheld,
fleeting time shall not bend thee,
death nor decay shalt thou see.

Michael Comyn

At the door toward the east
Are three trees of purple glass.
From their tops a flock of birds
Sing a sweetly drawn out song . . .

At the entrance to the enclosure is a tree
From whose branches there comes
Beautiful and harmonious music.
It is a tree of silver, which the sun illuminates.
It glistens like gold.

The Sick-Bed of Cuchulainn

My chair is in Caer Siddi,
Where no one is afflicted with age or illness . . .
It is surrounded by three circles of fire.
To the borders of the city come the ocean's flood,
A fruitful fountain flows before it,
Whose liquor is sweeter than the finest wine.

Taliesin

Even from these brief quotations it is possible to feel the wind of faerie blowing upon one's face. It has been said that once one has journeyed there, all one ever wants to do is return, so beautiful is that place and so joyful and welcoming its people. As a shaman you will visit it often, returning with news for the world outside.

THE SHAMAN'S COSMOS

By studying the many disparate elements within Celtic literature and myth, we can understand something of the cosmology which their shamans inhabited. It is not unlike many other such maps of the universe from different cultures, but it bears an unmistakable aura of 'Celticity'!

Firstly we see that the shaman moves in and through a three-tiered universe – consisting of Upperworld, Middleworld and Underworld – all connected by the Great Tree. (See Figure 2.)

The shaman sits at the centre, backing onto the Tree itself. It stretches above into the deepest reaches of space, where the stars are clustered in its branches and the sun and moon revolve through day and night, marking out the seasons of the year. All around are the eight cardinal points of the sacred wheel: the four directions north, south, east and west and the four cross-quarter points north-east, north-west, south-east and south-west.

In all directions from the centre stretches the Middleworld, the place where we live and breathe, but which at the same time possesses an Otherworldly dimension. The Otherworld shadows this realm constantly, overlapping with it in such a way that we are able at times to pass from one dimension to the other, if we have the keys and know the way. It is from here that the shamans begin their journeys, either by climbing the bole of the tree towards the Upperworld, or following it down into the Underworld.

The Upperworld is the place of stars, of criss-crossing influences, of deity, and of the changing focus of the inner and outer worlds. From it we can view the entire cosmos and move outward into it. For though the shaman's universe is small enough to fit within a hazelnut, it is also as vast as the widest stretch of our imaginations.

Below is the Root of the Tree, the Underworld realm where the spirits of earth and fire move and where sits the Lord of the Underworld. It is also the domain of the beasts, and of a stag-headed god who guards the Well of Segais, from which rise the seven rivers of life, coursing through the Underworld and spreading out and upward in a rainbow which grows to encircle the other worlds. Behind him is the massive figure of the Goddess of the Earth, a mighty and empowering figure carved out of living rock. Within the rainbow float, run or fly all the totem beasts and the spirits of air and water upon which the shaman calls. In the roof

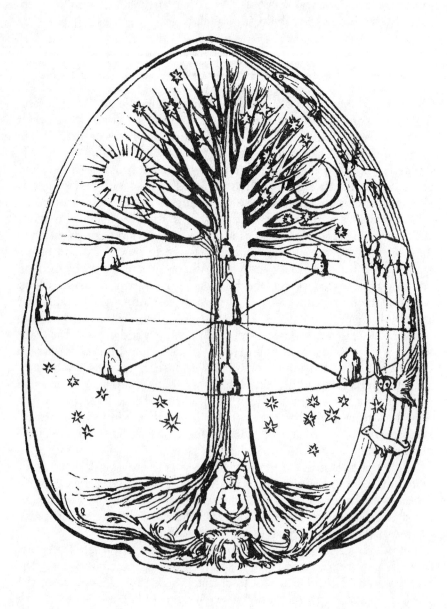

Figure 2. The Celtic Shaman's Universe

of the Underworld shine forth the stars of the earth, the crystals which empower and light this realm, and which mirror those of the firmament. From the Underworld come the teachings of the ancestors, the primal beings who are the founders of the Celtic race. Here lies the deepest layer of the shamanic tradition.

Thus are the three worlds linked, and all are perceived as growing within the shell of a single hazelnut positioned at the lip of the Well of Segais, from where, according to Celtic tradition, all knowledge comes. The shaman journeys to this point in search of wisdom and understanding; all things are linked together here, where all archetypal forms are to be found. Here is the reality of the shadow world we inhabit, containing the true aspects of all beings — animal, human and Otherworldly — which interact and change and affect each other throughout eternity. Here the shamans walk, between the worlds and in the worlds, striking deep into the heart of creation and discovering what place they and the people they serve hold within it.

Within the inner worlds the shamans cross great distances of both time and space. They may encounter a bewildering range of beings there — animals, birds, fish, gods, even abstract forces. From all of these they derive the information needed to guide, heal, or advise either themselves or those who consult them. Thus if a shaman requires information about whether it is advisable to cut down a tree in his own garden, or in a client's garden, he will probably enter the inner realm at the earthly level and, meeting there with the spirit of the tree, make known his wish. Or, if required to heal, he will visit the interior places from which it is possible to see more clearly the nature of sickness itself, and to find out from his helpers the best kind of cure.

Here *you* too will learn to travel, becoming in time familiar with the Many-coloured Lands outside the dimension of time and space as they are measured in this world. But before you can do so you must understand the shamanic orientations of your own dimensions, the Middleworld. Each of the fixed points here correlates with those of the Otherworld, and once you have mastered these, you are free to range still further afield.

A single glyph exists, common to almost every shamanic tradition in the world, and which appears carved upon stones all across the Celtic countries. This is the circled cross, sometimes augmented to become an eight-spoked wheel, and once you have understood its construction and the many qualities and correspondences which can be placed around and within it, you will have created a firm foundation from which to explore both upper and lower worlds (see Figure 4).

The abundance of this glyph reveals not only its importance to the

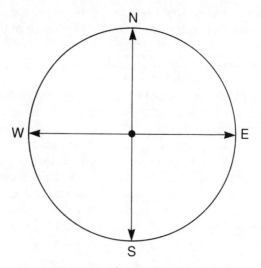

Figure 3. The Circled Cross

Celts, but also the way in which it reflects a natural order which is present in every dimension. This is the basic pattern of the four directions, augmented by the above and the below, which together constitute a map applicable in *all* worlds. The Celts saw the shape of the wheel in many things, as did many other early cultures. In a recent study of the symbol as it appears in archaeological and mythic sources, the Celtic scholar Miranda Green recognized literally hundreds of instances in which it appeared. Of course, not all of these are applicable to our present study, but the importance of the symbol to Celtic shamanism is undeniable.

It has long been accepted that the wheel appears most often as a representation of the circling of the seasons. Let us begin therefore from the same point, with the shape of the year.

THE CELTIC YEAR

Our Celtic ancestors divided the year into four quarters, roughly equivalent to the seasons of spring, summer, autumn and winter. The Celts were, of course, an agricultural people, and it was therefore important for them to recognize the passing of the seasons, and to honour the great days on which each was seen to begin. In ancient Ireland, for example, there were no individual names for the months, which took their titles from the four major festivals.

The four great festivals of the Celtic year are:

Imbolc (Time of Parturition/Lactation): 1 February
Beltaine (Bright Fire): 1 May
Lughnasadh (Lugh's Wedding-day): 1 August
Samhain (Summer's Death): 1 November

In fact, in accordance with Celtic tradition (which always placed night or darkness before day or light) each festival was seen as beginning on the evening of the previous day, so that the dates are sometimes given as 31 January, 30 April, 31 July and 31 October. Although the festivals are celebrated around the dates given here, they were not determined by the calendrical date, but by the manifestation of the seasons: thus, Beltaine would not have taken place until the May or hawthorn blossom was out. They would also have been celebrated at the time of the full-moon, since all festivals began at evening. The Celts reckoned the 'day' from evening to evening, not, as we do, from morning to morning.

Imbolc (Im'olk) marked the lessening of winter's grip and the coming of new life in the spring. It was the time of the birth of lambs, when ewes' milk flowed and all kinds of beginnings were celebrated. As this is a time of year when it is usually inadvisable to travel far, due to harsh weather conditions, this was very much a family festival, with young men and women making songs and vigils to the goddess Brighid, who was also the goddess of midwifery and fosterage. Many children may have been born at this time as the result of Beltaine the previous summer. Imbolc is the time for auguries concerning our destiny and direction during the coming year.

Beltaine (Bel'ta-na) marked the beginning of the summer and was one of the major gateways between the worlds: the period from Beltaine to Samhain was called *an ghrian mor*, 'the greater sun', while the period from Samhain to Beltaine was *an ghrian beag*, 'the lesser sun'. Beltaine was the time when animals were let out from the byres to eat the fresh spring grass; herds and flocks were driven between two fires in order to purify them of any diseases resulting from their winter incarceration. Remnants of many Celtic May-customs abound in Britain and Ireland, where villagers still choose May queens and dance about Maypoles. The gates of the Otherworld stood open at this time and it was considered lucky to seek the gifts of the *sidhe*, the folk of the Other-world, by rising early in the morning: gifts were granted more easily to the young and beautiful. Beltaine is the time for coming into our strength and realizing our desires.

Lughnasadh (Loo'nas'a) marked the time of harvest, of tribal get-together, of horse-fairs, arbitrations, trial-marriages and hard business deals. There were also ritual games, combative bouts, horse-racing and possibly the choosing of the tribe's *tanaiste*, its approved successor to the chieftain or monarch. There is a sense of sacrifice at this time of year, as the crops are brought in: the state and condition of the harvest was representative of the reign of the current leader. If his reign had been poor, the land would reflect this lack of commitment, and it would be time to consider finding a new, more able, ruler. This festival provides an opportunity for assessing our responsibilities and commitments.

Samhain (Sa'wen) marked the Celtic new year. It may seem strange to start a new year at this 'dead' time, but the growing season really begins with the winter sowing of crops, thereby implanting new life in the dormant fields. It was a time of communing with the ancestors, a feature which Celtic Christians incorporated into the festival of All Souls, a direct legacy of the ancient festival. Storytelling began in earnest during the long, dark, winter nights; many of these tales would have been ghost-stories about the Otherworld, whose gates stood wide open at this time, allowing the dead to walk abroad. Only those in disguise would venture out on this night to confuse the *sidhe*, the Faerie kind and the feared, though revered ancestors: a custom which has been passed down to us as Mischief Night, Hallow'een and 'trick or treat'. Samhain is a good time for recycling, transforming or throwing away whatever is stale or outworn.

This divided the year into four, though there is also a 'hidden' division into halves, dark and light. Many of the tales emanating from these focal points in the passage of the year reflect this: for example, the champions of winter and summer do battle every year for possession of the maiden of spring, a custom still current at the end of the nineteenth century.
    The year is further subdivided by the solstices and equinoxes:

Spring equinox: 21 March
Midsummer: 21 June
Autumn equinox: 21 September
Midwinter: 21 December

These Sun festivals, together with the Celtic Festivals, and establish a powerful network of reference-points which help orient shamans who work with the symbolism of the wheel. But these are only a few of the possibilities which exist. A complex web of correlations can be placed upon the wheel, which embraces so many levels of meaning that it forms the centre of the shamanic cosmology. Not only the natural events of the year, but also mythological events, qualities, and happenings of inner significance can be added, building up to a highly complex whole. The number of references which can be placed around the wheel are almost endless: significant dates, colours, winds, plants, animals, totems, birds and fish are but a few of the possibilities. With increased use the changing pattern of the natural world, and of the relationships between the inner and outer realms, becomes more and more apparent.

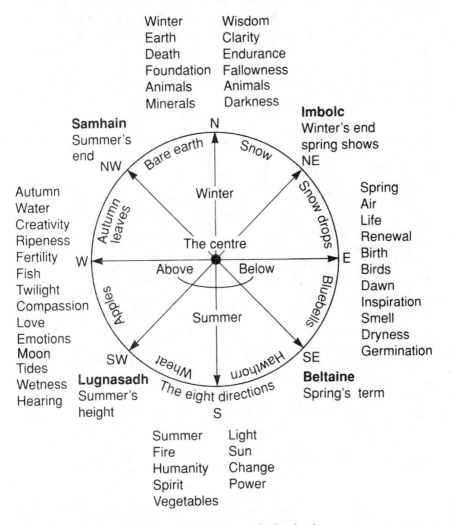

Figure 4: The Eight-spoked Wheel

If we start with a simple diagram, we can build up some of the correlations already discussed, as well as others which will occur as you study the wheel more deeply.

THE SACRED CALENDAR

Ideally you should be looking at ways of working with the ancient sacred sites of the land, which still retain so much of the power and energy of the native shamans. This will not always be possible, of course, and you must not think that your work will suffer unduly as a result. You can operate just as well in your own front room as at a stone circle or chambered howe; it is what you bring to your *own* circle which is important. *All* parts of the earth are sacred. And wherever you decide to practise, you will need to orient yourself properly at the start.

In this respect it is important to learn the structure which underpins the sacred year. The ancient peoples were far more in tune with this than we will ever be, and thus we need constant reminders of *where we stand* in relation to the seasons, the phases of the moon, the position of the sun and so on.

The Celts had a highly complex calendrical system, based on the cycles of sun and moon. Traces of this have been discovered among both literature and artefacts, in particular a Gaulish calendar found at Coligney, inscribed on sheets of bronze, which gives a remarkable insight into the nature of this system.

As already mentioned, the year is divided into the four seasons, which are further subdivided. Each of these divisions, which do not correspond exactly to our modern months, indicate both the changing agricultural year and the cycles of sun and moon. The original names and their meanings, together with approximate timings, as given on the Coligney calendar, are as follows:

Samionos	Seed fall	Oct/Nov
Dumannios	Darkest depths	Nov/Dec
Riuros	Cold-time	Dec/Jan
Anagantios	Stay-home time	Jan/Feb
Ogronios	Time of ice	Feb/Mar
Cutios	Time of winds	Mar/Apr
Giamonios	Shoots-show	Apr/May
Samivisionos	Time of brightness	May/Jun
Equos	Horse-time	Jun/Jul
Elembiuos	Claim-time	Jul/Aug

| *Edrinios* | Arbitration-time | Aug/Sep |
| *Cantlos* | Song-time | Sep/Oct |

These reflect clearly the passage of the year, which as a shaman you will need to know intimately, so study the list and try to memorize it. It may help to make a shamanic calendar by drawing a circle and dividing it up into twelve segments. Write the names of the months around the outside and then fill in the segments with a brief description of the natural world as you observe it. (Some of the appellations, such as Claim-time, Arbitration-time or Horse-time, are less relevant to us than to our Celtic forbears. Try to find new names to adapt the calendar for your own use.)

Due to the careless and selfish manner in which most of our world behaves, the seasons today are in a state of flux. One of the primary tasks of the shaman or shamanka is to understand this and to try to do whatever is necessary to improve the situation. It may well be too late to put right all the harm we have done to our mother the earth, but we can still say that we are sorry and work towards a happier, more balanced world (see also Chapter 6).

The Coligny calendrical system can be adapted in an endless number of ways. It can become a tree calendar, based on the names of the sacred trees discussed in Chapter 7. You can also create a totemic moon calendar, indicated by association with certain birds, animals and fish (see Chapter 3).

THE CENTRE

But it is not sufficient merely to learn the directions, the placing and distribution of elements and so forth around the wheel. It is necessary to establish within yourself an *inner* cosmology of which you are always aware at a certain level, and to which you can relate at any given moment.

Before you can begin to explore the shape of the wheel, you need to establish a sacred centre within yourself. Here you can learn to stand still (truly still), and regard the passage of time and events in relation to yourself. At the centre time stops. From this point your place in the wheel, or the circle of the world can be measured; the Sacred Circle becomes a working model of the shamanic universe which you may learn to traverse at will, whether physically or spiritually.

As already shown, the shamanic cosmos consists of three levels, connected by a central stem, sometimes known as the Great Tree, sometimes as the Pole of the Worlds. Thus the bard Taliesin refers to 'the great pole, which connects earth and heaven'; while the story of the great Irish hero Cuchulainn describes how, when his last and greatest battle was going badly, Cuchulainn strapped himself to a stone mono-lith, which represented the central backbone of creation, and drew strength and support from it. Thus, when we are supported by the central pole of the heavens we can look outward in any of the directions and place any quality we wish upon them, allowing us to 'see' their interrelationships with increasing clarity. As Joseph Epes Brown puts it: 'Without such ritual fixing of a centre there can be no circumference. And with neither centre nor circumference where does a person stand?' (*The Roots of Renewal*).

The ritual navel of the earth and of the shaman is also the true centre and, in order to understand your own place within the order of creation, you need to position yourself at its ritual centre. Thus, when a shaman or shamanka stands at the central point of their circle, and faces one of the directions, he or she sees not just the section of sky or earth above or beneath them, not the wall before their eyes, but also the metaphysi-cal possibilities, relationships and correlations of which they are aware.

This can be represented as in Figure 5.

To be conscious of the central pole behind you is an important aspect of inner orientation, as well as being very useful in a difficult situation. If, for example, you are facing an adversary of any kind — whether physical or spiritual — you can draw upon the supporting strength of the pole. The following technique is designed both as an empowering exercise and also as a practical example of the way the symbolism becomes real when it is worked with properly.

The Pole

Imagine that the pole of the heavens is actually passing through you, up your spinal column, strengthening and supporting you at the same time . . . You can draw upon the power of the pole, which connects earth and sky, according to your needs. All shamans and their power helpers pass up and down this pole continually, and so you can call on many kinds of help. After you have obtained your own power helpers (see Chapter 4) you will be able to ask them for assistance. At this stage it is generally sufficient to be simply aware of the support at your back, and the strength available to give you the necessary power to get through the immediate problem.

By combining the concepts of the wheel and the centre, or Great Tree,

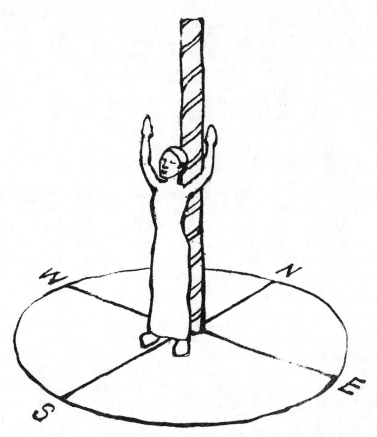

Figure 5. The Pole of the Heavens

you can further extend your understanding of the shamanic cosmos. Like the wheel the tree is a symbolic reality, which helps you gain access to the various totem powers, gods and beings with which you will work. But it is important to realize that these images and symbols are only there to help you orient yourself. If you enter the Otherworld expecting to see a three-dimensional version of Figure 2 you will be severely disappointed. This is simply one way of looking at the inner worlds which reflects the experiences of shamans from many parts of the world, and is based on personal exploration. The reality is much more. The Otherworld is neither an archetype produced by the unconscious mind, nor a product of the imagination. Once you have journeyed there you will understand for yourself how real it is – in some ways more real than the manifest world in which we live.

As the unknown poet who composed *The Voyage of Bran* wrote:

Speckled salmon leap from the womb
Of the white sea, on which thou lookst:
They are calves, they are coloured lambs
With friendliness, without mutual slaughter.

Though but one chariot-rider is seen
In Mag Mell of many flowers,
There are many steeds on its surface,
Though them thou seest not.

Trans. K. Meyer

When you begin to journey into these realms you will quickly become responsive to innerworld reality. This corresponds in some degree to the outline of the Celtic cosmos described above. It is not yet time for you to undertake such a journey, and what follows is an example of the kind of vision which might be experienced. It should not be seen as a valid substitute for your own journeying, merely as a starting point from which you may make further explorations in due course.

A Vision of the Tree

Beneath the stone the tree struggles to be free, pushes at the dark unyielding granite until it cracks, splits apart and falls in rubble on the earth. Released, the tree climbs, putting forth branches and twigs, dancing in bold green leaf and bright new bark. Upward and upward it climbs until, taller now than the mountain crags, it pierces through the clouds. Beyond, all is quiet. Not even birds sing; only the wind soughs in its branches. But still the tree grows, upward and onward, until it reaches the heights of heaven and knocks upon the secret door of the upper world . . .

Far below, the shaman hears the rustle of the leaves and the voice of the tree speaks to him, calling him to climb, to share the tree's view of the world. And so he begins to climb, hand over hand, up the tree. It is like a ladder that stretches up forever into the sky. Below the level of the clouds the shaman pauses, looking outwards across the curve of the bright world. He sees humanity in its restricting bubble: being born, living, loving and dying. He sees wars break out and end: pestilence and famine stalk the land. And, beneath it all, he hears the voice of the earth cry out in agony as more of its forests are cut down and its rivers and seas polluted. Even the air is filled with the reek of burning . . .

Shivering, the shaman climbs on, through the clouds and out into a night sky filled with stars. Looking up in wonder he sees an endless universe of worlds laid out upon the fabric of the heavens, and there, amid the turning and circling worlds, he sees the gods and spirits of the air, and the creatures of the earth going to and fro on many errands.

He communicates with some of these beings, listening closely to their answers. Often they tell him of the dangers faced by all humans in the world, and of the sorrow felt by those who move above the hoop of the earth. Then, feeling again the pull of the world, the shaman begins his descent. He climbs for many miles down the pole of the heavens, the tree that grows forever at the centre of creation, until at last he stands again on the warm earth, the breathing mother of all living things. Above him the tree stretches, its branches offering shelter to those who struggle to live beneath it in peace and harmony. Slowly, the shaman lays his hand upon the great trunk, feels the strength flowing through it. And he smiles then, knowing the power which touches all who walk the shaman's path and who are willing that the world should grow green again, and that all who live upon it should be in harmony with all life . . .

This vision contains references to concepts which will be dealt with later on, but it will give you an idea of what lies before you. For the moment, it is time to continue our exploration of the wheel and its correlations. To do this you will need to construct your own sacred space.

The Sacred Circle

First choose a place, outside if possible, though indoors will work just as well. Collect together a total of seventeen stones, five slightly larger than the rest. Now meditate and centre yourself as described in Chapter 1 until you reach a point of stillness within from which you can reach out and touch the mysterious whispering threads which bind the universe together. Now take one of the bigger stones, which will represent the centre, and set it in place, saying as you do:

I do this to honour the earth
which is the centre of my life.

Take time to think about all that this represents: stability, strength of purpose, directness of will, the foundation of the hearth upon the earth.

Now take the other four larger stones and go to each of the four cardinal points in turn, beginning with the east. When you have set each stone in place, take time to contemplate what each represents before moving on to the next one.

East has air, spring, new beginnings, new skills and fortunes, inspiration, renewal, dawn, birds, dryness.

South has fire, summer, light, changing ways, the burning away of old notions and received ideas, growth, dreams, humanity, sight.

West has water, autumn, creativity, fertility, compassion, twilight, love, tides, fish, inner purpose and the ability to grow wise in ways old and new.

North has earth, winter, strength, wisdom, clarity of perception, cold, the crystalline world, the animal kingdom, minerals and darkness.

Consider each of these things, and other notions that will occur to you. See how they relate to you as you stand at that quarter. What things have you begun, or will you begin, in the spring tide? Did they reach fruition in the summer and continue around till autumn? Did they grow to wisdom and come to full-term in the winter? What season draws you most strongly? Which of the elemental kingdoms do you resonate with best? Which animal, bird or fish represents you? These are all things which you will need to know, so take your time and learn to 'feel' the quality of the direction you are facing. As you lay each stone in place say quietly:

I do this to honour the [quarter in question]
which is to me [whatever you perceive as most effective].

Now, when you are ready, take up the stones which will represent the four great festivals: Imbolc, Beltaine, Lughnasadh and Samhain. Consider what these mean to you, their mythical resonances; they can also be seen as representing the four ages of humanity:

Imbolc = child
Beltaine = youth
Lughnasadh = adult
Samhain = elder

When you are ready, position the stones with care and intent.

Now it is time to lay out the eight remaining stones which mark out the solar/lunar months. Begin with Samionos (Seed fall); next Dumannios (Darkest depths); then Riuros (Cold-time); Anagantios (Stay-home time); Ogronios (Time of ice); Cutios (Time of winds); Giamonios (Shoots-show); Samivisionos (Time of brightness); Equos (Horse-time); Elembiuos (Claim-time); Edrinios (Arbitration-time); Cantlos (Song-time). Lay out the stones at intervals as shown in Figure 6 and as you do so consider the qualities of the month, the beings associated with it and any dimension you have attributed to it (until you have worked these out to conform to your own pattern, use those given in the diagram on p. 41.)

Now seat yourself at the centre of your circle and meditate upon all that you have done. Try to be aware of the qualities you have invoked at each quarter. You would normally begin a piece of work at this point, so in this instance go to each quarter again and thank the energies and qualities (seen or unseen) which have helped you to establish your first circle. Depending on whether you have been working indoors or outside you can either leave the stones in place (a permanent circle is ideal) or take them up and place them upon your shrine (see Chapter 4).

Thus you can orient your shamanic work around the year, celebrating the seasons in a natural and rhythmic manner. The direction in which you face will be to some extent dictated by the kind of work you are

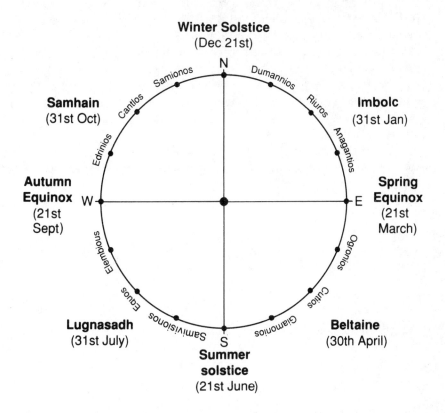

Figure 6. The Wheel of the Year

engaged in: north when the work is earth/body related; south: fire/mind related, west: water/emotion related, east: air/spirit related.

With this pattern established, allowing you to set up your sacred circle anywhere and at any time, you can begin to explore the shaman's world. Other qualities, elements, and correspondences can be placed around the circle, represented by the stones, and these will be explored in the next two chapters. This will form the basis of all the work you will do in the first months of your shamanic practice and requires all your dedication and concentration.

You may feel at this point that there is one very important dimension which is missing: the beings, gods and goddesses, which also have their places upon the wheel. These will be dealt with later, and have been left out of this initial building of the wheel deliberately. When you come to invite the mighty innerworld forces into your sacred circle, or travel forth to discover the totem beasts and power animals, you need to be certain that your circle is well contracted, laid out with thought and intention, and strong enough to contain the energies with which you will be working. It is essential that you work as much as possible with the shape of the year, and that you learn to be sensitive to the seasons and qualities you begin to discover for yourself. At that point you will be ready to explore the upper and lower worlds, so until then be patient and work hard at the wheel.

Having thus begun the map of the inner cosmos through which the Celtic shaman moves, it is time to discuss the beings you will encounter on your many journeys into the inner realms.

3 Companions of Power

Then there grew upon my head
Two antlers with three score points.
So that I am rough and grey in shape
After my age has changed from
    feebleness.'

Tuan Mac Cairell

TOTEM BEASTS

AMONG PEOPLE WHO POSSESS a more or less unbroken shamanic tradition, it is still commonly held that just as one is born with certain innate gifts – the ability to sing, a talent for painting or sculpting, the gift of languages – so everyone has a spirit being attached to them from birth. This being is generally referred to as a totem beast, and it acts as a guardian and guide both in the inner realms and in the physical world. It may take the form of an unseen companion, or of an animal or bird or fish.

We are familiar enough with the concept of the 'invisible friend' possessed by most children at an early age; the spirit being is much like this. And, in the same way that most children lose all awareness of their unseen companion as they grow older, so do we forget (if we ever knew it to begin with) our totem. The shaman, on the other hand, at least in a tribal setting, is trained to retain this awareness.

Even the most unaware person today retains at least *some* latent memory of such a totem beast in their consciousness, and this can be activated without much difficulty. The following journey is intended to help you to discover your totem beast. It is included here with the permission of Caitlín Matthews, who first devised it. It has been used frequently both with individuals and larger groups, always successfully, and with a degree of power which continues to surprise us.

The plan is to discover the identity of your totem beast, which may be seen as representing either you as an individual, or the group to which you may belong (as in the Clan of the Bear, or the Dog, or the Stag). It is probable that you already have such a guide; it is a representation of your personal shamanic identity and of the qualities you mediate to the rest of the world. It may be kept secret as part of your inner, shamanic name (see p. 70), or displayed openly on a shield. But remember that you do not choose your totem beast; it is more true to say that it chooses you.

For the exercise which follows you will need to change your consciousness as described in Chapter 1. There are many different ways of doing this, one of which is the use of the drum, as suggested here, and techniques for drumming are discussed in Chapter 6. Until you have mastered these, and possibly obtained your own drum, you should use one of the recommended tapes listed at the end of this book – 'Shamanizing' by John and Caitlín Matthews includes various rhythms with explanations of their use.

The Totem Beast

Get someone to drum for you or, if this is not possible, put on one of the recommended drumming tapes found in the resource list at the back of this book. As you listen to the drum imagine you are climbing down a great tree, which grows not only up above the earth but also down into it. This time you are going to be climbing under the earth. The tree will seem to go on forever, but you will reach the bottom eventually, and there you will see a clearing in a forest, and at the foot of the tree you will see a figure with antlers, seated. He will be strong and dark and powerful, but not unfriendly. He is called the wild herdsman, and he is the guardian of all beasts. When he sees you he will bang the trunk of the tree with a huge club, and a beast will come out of the trees towards you. This will be your creature. It can be anything from a mouse to a golden eagle or a domestic cat. Whatever it is, greet it with friendship and welcome it into you. It will merge with your body; when it has done so you can begin to climb back up the tree. The timing of this will vary from person to person. It may take anything from ten to forty minutes, and you should try to time your drumming tape accordingly, or tell whoever is drumming that you will make a sign when you are ready to return to normal consciousness. At this point he or she should increase the tempo to bring you back up to the surface. Then you should get up and dance your animal, and give it a voice, where appropriate, as loud and as long as you like. Or you can be silent – it's up to you. The only important thing is that you allow the totem being to express itself as strongly as it will.

Repeat this exercise as often as you feel is necessary to establish a really strong inner rapport with your totem animal. In particular, dance it as often as you can. This means imitating the movements of your particular creature as far as humanly possible, which keeps the animal close and subtle within you. At random moments during the day try to 'see' with your animal's eyes, and 'feel' with its senses, which enhance your own. Singing songs of and to your animal is also an excellent idea. These may well come from the creature itself, or may be devised by you, as in the following, non-specific, example.

> I am the bright one
> I am the bright one
> With shoes of fire.
> I walk in the night
> I dance in the day
> In a hidden manner
> Till I come with dawn
> And with dawn leap forth
> Into the day.
> I am the bright one
> I am the bright one
> With shoes of fire.

You will soon learn a great deal from your inner companion. Follow its lead and be aware of its intelligence, and you will be astonished at what it can teach you. Often, answers to questions will come in the form of complex riddles rather than direct answers. These generally yield up their meaning with a little meditation or reliance on intuition. They are a part of the way in which the totem being can help you in all kinds of situations: you may turn to your animal for help towards self-healing, and as a general guide through the rougher waters of experience. You may have more than one animal as time goes on, sometimes several at one time; or perhaps just one that remains with you over a longer period.

It may be that you will encounter an animal which you fear or hate. After a totem beast workshop I gave recently I was approached by someone who was greatly concerned that the creature she had encountered was one she found so loathsome that even to look at it made her feel physically ill. I suggested that she had to face the creature — I did not ask what it was — and that to come to terms with it would help her to cope with some problem deep within her. Not every totem beast will seem either friendly or likeable, and you will need to learn to accept this in your own way; you will derive great benefit from learning more about yourself and your inner abilities, fears and doubts.

If you are concerned that your totem beast might not be suitable, ask it questions. It may be, for instance, that you are not yet ready to accept the gifts it has to offer. Like Beauty, who came to love and trust the Beast, you should always follow your heart and your instinct. If you feel uncertain about the trustworthiness of your animal helper, ask it to show you a vision of something that means a great deal to you. Once back in everyday consciousness, check that vision against your own under-standing and see what this tells you. Remember that if you continue to feel uncomfortable with the totem animal you can journey again and see if another, more appropriate being, comes forward. That may be the one for you.

If you decide to carry some token of your totem with you, such as a feather, a bone, or a tuft of fur, you should ask leave of it while in trance-state. You will be given permission to take a feather, a skull or a piece of hide to carry in your crane bag (see Chapter 6). If you make no conscious effort to find such items you will find that they come to you. You may be walking in the countryside and discover what you require, or else a local junk shop will yield up the desired token. However, it is important to understand the ethics involved in using such animal products. Owning or wearing such things is not necessarily a bad thing; the way in which they are acquired requires more consideration. Finding naturally generated objects such as skulls, bones or feathers is one thing, but going out and looking for an animal to kill is clearly another. If you feel uncomfortable with the idea of owning such objects there are alternatives in the form of artefacts, carvings or jewellery.

You can add your own details to these items. For example, you might have a raven for your totem, and find a raven's feather. Try binding some tufts of sheep's wool to it with red thread. You thus have a token displaying the three sacred colours, black, white and red. Now meditate upon this – on the raven as a bird that feeds on carrion, the sheep as mother, and the fact that one preys upon the other and scavenges its dead body. Within such elements lies a world of insight which can transform the way you perceive both the natural world and your own life.

POWER ANIMALS

In addition to the totem beast, which can remain with you throughout your life, or at least for a long period of time, you will acquire certain power animals at different times. These are similar in kind to the totem beasts but tend to be called upon under special circumstances, such as during a crisis or in the event of a particular life challenge requiring more than usual amounts of energy, skill or wisdom. We may select a power animal specifically because of its innate skills. Unlike the totem beasts, power animals do not represent you either to the ancestors (see also Chapter 9) or to the gods.

Throughout the literature of shamanism the concept of the helping animal is mentioned repeatedly. In each case the shaman possesses a non-physical inner helper in the form of an animal which provides strength, intuition, and understanding of events from a different point of view from that of the shaman. Sometimes there is a call upon the speed, strength, and endurance of the helper, as well as the keenness of animal senses. At other times the animals may tell shamans things which they could not know for themselves.

At one time humanity and the animal kingdom were more closely related than at present, allowing better inter-species communication (the same may, incidentally, be said of human and Otherworldly beings); but gradually the differences became greater and the gaps between the species widened. Shamans have kept open the avenues of communication by working with inner-world creatures in the shape of animal, bird, or fish. They have learned to adopt the skills and sometimes the shapes of the creatures, borrowing their strength, swiftness, keen-sightedness and cunning as adjuncts to their own lives and abilities.

In each case it is the *spirit* of the creature which is being contacted, perhaps even the spirit which represents *all* the species in question. I remember being asked to get rid of some harvest mice which were plaguing a friend's house, and I did this by making an inner journey to contact the spirit of a harvest mouse. I asked it to tell its cousins to depart, and the mice were not seen again. I believe that this goes some way towards explaining the constant references to shamans possessing spirit helpers. These may not always take animal form, but may have the appearance of long-dead ancestors, or even heroic or mythic beings (see also Chapter 9). In effect the shaman makes a home for the spirit being, whether in animal or supra-human form.

Many Celtic heroes had shamanic abilities which derived from their personal totems: far-sightedness, precognition, great strength etc., and these were seen as deriving from totem beasts or animal helpers, often born at the same time in the physical world. The Irish hero Cuchulainn, for example, had an extraordinary relationship with a horse which foaled at the time of his birth.

There are many other examples of animal helpers in Celtic mythology, in particular in the case of the shaman-bard Taliesin. During his initiation he was changed into the forms of various creatures, from each of which he learned something of value. In the story of Culhwch and Olwen, from Welsh tradition, the hero, engaged on a quest, receives help from a number of magical creatures, each one older than the next, who together assist him in the release of the child-god Mabon (see Matthews: *Mabon & the Mysteries of Britain*).

There are a number of valuable things to be learned from stories of this kind. In the first we see the shaman in a symbiotic relationship with animal, bird and fish, each one introducing him to another element. In the second we see the hero being helped by Otherwordly animals — again birds, beasts and fish — to release what we may see, on one level, as the imprisoned child. Indeed, this second scenario has been used, with evident success, in modern therapeutic work (see the work of Ian Rees in Stewart, 1990), and while this is an instance of a specifically psychological use of magical forms, it does show the relationship of the shamanic power animal in the quest for individual healing.

It is important also to remember that these are not some cardboard cut-out or visualization: within their own world, they all have the qualities of real animals. The power animals possess all the qualities of their outerworld kin, following the behavioural patterns of their species. The only point of difference is in that they are able to relate to their human companion at a far deeper level and with greater parity than would normally be the case, even with the strongest master–pet relationship. It is this rapport which enables the shaman to learn from his or her animals at an astonishingly deep level.

The shaman's ability to assume the form of animal, bird or fish, as well as to empathize with apparently non-sentient objects such as swords, harp-strings or stones, is all part of native shamanic practices. The enhanced senses possessed by wild creatures can be of enduring importance and value to all who seek to follow the shaman's path, and so shamans frequently adopt the form, or use the gifts, of their power animal to enhance and empower their practice.

The energies of all creatures are present within each of us already; we have simply to tap into them by working with the power animals who represent the speed and grace, the beauty and delicacy of each one. Taliesin's final transformation is one of rebirth, and in a very real way all such transformative exercises are a continuing reawakening to our own potential. If you have difficulty finding power animals of your own you should take a journey down the tree, and ask your totem beast to find a power animal for you. One should soon appear, though you may well be surprised at what it is. Often it is the most unexpected creature, though it is usually the one you require, even if you did not realize it!

The next exercise, concerning shapeshifting, will give you some idea of the range of possibilities offered by your power animal relationship. As well as broadening the quality of your awareness, it will help you to make contact with the spirit of the creature you have chosen to work with. In one of the most extraordinary of Taliesin's poems he says:

> I have been a sow, I have been a buck.
> I have been a sage, I have been a snout,
> I have been a horn, I have been a wild sow,
> I have been a shout in battle,
> I have been a gushing torrent,
> I have been a wave on the long shore.
> I have been a gentle rain.
> I have been a speckled cat in a forked tree.
> I have been a circle, I have been a head,
> I have been a goat in an elder tree.

Here lies one of the most important clues to the purpose of shapeshifting. It does not, of course, imply that you 'physically' change your shape; rather that you are identifying with the creature in question. Essentially it gives you an ever-deepening awareness of the world about you. By identifying with animal, bird or fish (or with the plants, minerals or elements themselves) at a deep level, you are in fact coming to know the particular totem in a way that no amount of study or observation could provide. Shifting your shape gives you a sense of 'otherness', of not being yourself; a fresh perspective on the world. It is thus that some of the most valuable lessons of shamanism are learned.

Shapeshifting

To begin this exercise decide what bird or beast, or fish or fowl, you wish to become. Think carefully and consider what aspect of the creature attracts you. Is it its grace, its strength, its swiftness, its keenness of sight or hearing, its ability to move through the air or in the water, or its connection with the Otherworld? When you have decided, find a picture of the creature or, if you can, go and look at one; if you have access to a wild place where your animal is found go there, wait and watch; avoid zoos, which have entirely the wrong atmosphere. If you are at home find a space, and make sure you will not be interrupted for at least thirty minutes. Then begin your meditation. If outdoors go directly into a concentrated state, working as hard as possible to feel the creature you have chosen: How does it use its senses? What are its feelings? What scents and sounds does it hear? If you are indoors, begin by visualizing the creature's habitat: woodland, river, mountaintop or whatever. Then begin to feel yourself as present there, not in your own familiar form but in that of the creature you have chosen. You may find it helpful to assume the nearest bodily posture to that of the creature. If it is a bird, squat on your haunches, rotate your arms and shoulders, tuck your head down, feel yourself preparing to fly. If you choose a fish, lie on the floor with feet close together and arms at your sides and try moving forward as though through water. Repeat your sensory exploration of your new environment.

When you have worked at this for a time, begin to make a chant, invoking the spirit of the creature in question. An example follows:

> Spirit of the stag be mine.
> Power of the stag be mine.
> Strength of the stag be mine.
> Endurance of the stag be mine.
>
> Spirit of the fox be mine.
> Cunning of the fox be mine.
> Swiftness of the fox be mine.
> Strength of the fox be mine.
>
> Spirit of the eagle be mine.
> Grace of the eagle be mine.
> Sight of the eagle be mine.
> Might of the eagle be mine.

Repeat this over and over steadily (if you have a partner get him or her to drum an appropriate rhythm for the creature you have chosen), all the while keeping its image in your mind, using every faculty to its limits. After a while you should begin to merge with the creature, to feel its spirit coming to life within you. Take your time with this exercise and let the strength of the creature run within you for as long as you need. Repeat as often as is necessary, until gradually, over the weeks, you begin to be able to invoke the presence of the creature at a moment's notice. New strengths and abilities will come to you, and you will experience a new understanding of the world which can be of help in many different circumstances or situations in your life.

THE TOTEMS

We have already touched on the importance of journeying to inner worlds, and being able to orient yourself when there. One of the principle purposes of the power animal or totem beast is to help bring this about. Once you begin to work with such inner beings, you will discover that the Otherworld possesses not only a tremendous sense of reality but also rules of its own. In an earlier book (*The Western Way*

Vol. 1) I included an exercise called 'The Two Trees', which derived from a group working the ancient native spirituality of the British Isles. The exercise contained a gateway into another world the extent of which neither I, nor anyone I know of who has entered it, has ever gauged. One person, who already had considerable experience of magical work, telephoned me a few weeks after I had conveyed the meditation to her. 'This thing does itself', she said, and went on to describe the way in which the inner scenario would continue to change direction, even after quite lengthy periods in which she had stopped the meditation. The scenario was always true to its point of origin, though it often seemed to have moved on in time or place. The same guides and guardians reappeared, as did other characters, building up a complex system. The inner world of the totems and power animals is much the same as this, though of course they are not the only denizens of the many-coloured land. You may leave it alone for weeks, even months, and on returning you will find that this inner life has been continuing without you.

There follows a list of animals and their correlations to help you recognize the kind of qualities you will be looking for in your own totem or power animal. This is not a complete list, but is made up of those creatures which most often appear in the Celtic stories and which possess the strongest energies and powers. I have given their names in Scots and Irish Gaelic or Welsh, in the belief that in a Celtic scenario they respond more readily when addressed by these names.

The Salmon (Brionnfhionn)
This creature probably appears more often than any other in the Celtic world. It is always associated with wisdom and the acquiring of knowledge. Sometimes this is said to be because it swims in the pool beside which grow the Nine Hazels of Wisdom. Nuts fall from the trees into the water and are eaten by the salmon, which is then able to transmit the wisdom to individuals. The Salmon of Assaroe is one of the most famous fish in the Celtic world – it was at least as old as time, and had seen most of the comings and goings of mankind. The hero-shaman Fionn Mac Cumhail acquired all his wisdom by partaking of a salmon which he was cooking for the Druid Fintan.

The Deer or Stag (Abhach, Sailetheach)
The importance of the deer among the Celts is testified not only by the number of appearances it makes in the mythology, but also by the astonishing number of words used to describe it. It was always seen as a magical creature, which could lead one into the Otherworld, and often

appears in the guise of a beautiful woman who can take the shape of the deer at will. The hero Fionn's Otherworldly wife was called Sabha, and took on a deer's form when she departed from the mortal world. There is evidence of the existence of a deer cult, in which the animal was worshipped as a goddess. The deer thus represents travel to the Hollow Hills or the faerie realm, shapeshifting (the perception of the world from different viewpoints), and the natural deer-like qualities of grace, swiftness and keen scent.

The Horse (Cab-all)

Horses were always important to the Celts and one of their greatest taboos was against the eating of horse-flesh, or their deliberate maiming. Thus in the *Mabinog* of Branwen, when the troublesome Efnissien cut off the eyelids, lips and tails of the visiting Irish king's horses he sparked off a war. The shape of the horse etched into the chalk of White Horse Hill in Wiltshire has long stood as an image of power to all who see it. Aside from its obvious speed and stamina another aspect of the horse as totem is its ability to know the ways into the Otherworld, and to be a good and faithful guide therein.

The Hawk (Aracos)

The most famous hawk in Celtic myth is the Hawk of Achill. In a marvellous riddling dialogue with the poet Fintan, it reveals a breadth of knowledge stretching back almost to the beginning of time. The hawk thus stands for the far-reaching memory which is such an important part of shamanic skill. With the hawk as your companion on an inner journey you will travel far, perhaps even to the realm of the ancestors themselves, who hold all knowledge in their souls and may choose to share it with those who know the proper way to ask.

The Eagle (Iolair)

Eagles appear throughout Celtic tradition and as might be expected they carry the qualities of swiftness, keen sight and magic. There exists a dialogue between the hero Arthur and an eagle – his nephew Ewilod in bird form – in which the eagle displays a depth of wisdom and a knowledge of the Otherworld. Another famous example is the Eagle of Cilgwry, whose power leads to the finding of the Celtic god Mabon. In the Irish text *The Voyage of Maelduin*, an ancient eagle renews itself in a lake, an act representative of the renewal of wisdom in every generation.

The eagle thus becomes a powerful ally when venturing into fresh territory.

The Sow and the Boar (Airc and Bacrie)

Both were considered to be powerful Otherworldly beasts. The sow was closely associated with the goddess Ceridwen, who was the initiatrix of poets and seers, and whose shamanic teachings brought forth Taliesin. There was also the sow Hen-Wen, believed to possess great wisdom and knowledge from having eaten the beech-nuts which fell from the Trees of Wisdom. The same monstrous sow was said to have dropped from her womb such staple provisions as corn and bees, as well as the Cath Palug (see *Cat*). The boar, in various forms, haunts Celtic literature as a creature of great totemic power and strength. The terrible 'Twrch Trwyth' was hunted by Arthur in the Mabinog of Culhwch and Olwen, while in another tale he pursued Hen Wen herself. In Irish tradition the White Boar of Marvan inspired his master to write music and poetry. Merlin also held dialogues with a 'little pig' during periods of inspired vision.

The Blackbird (Druid-dhubh)

A bird long associated with magic and the ability to pass into the Otherworld. As its Gaelic name suggests it was also associated with the Druids, while still others identified it with the Birds of Rhiannon. These birds, whose song could put people to sleep or enchant them outside time, sang above the island of Gwales, where Bran the Blessed and his seven followers remained in a state of suspended life for seventy-two years, during which time they grew no older nor were aware of the passage of time. The blackbird is thus able to impart deep secrets of the Otherworld and to transport the listener to another place, as at twilight when it sings its mystical melody at the time of the between-lights.

The Crow and the Raven (Badb and Bran)

Though the crow was seen as a bird of ill-omen, and as betokening the Irish war-goddesses Macha, Badb, and Morrigan, it was also acknowledged for its skill, cunning and single-mindedness. It is a bringer of knowledge, though not always the kind the hearer might wish. As a companion in the Otherworld it is wise and knowledgeable, though sometimes tricky. Likewise the raven; as well as being the terrible stalker of the battlefield, it was recognized as an oracular bird, given to providing omens, though it too has a dubious reputation. Treat with care.

The Cat (Caoit)

Cats appear several times in Celtic myth, notably in the *Voyage of Maelduin* where the voyagers encounter an innocent-seeming kitten leaping to and fro on the tops of four pillars. When one of the crew tries to steal some treasure which is nearby the cat becomes a fiery arrow and reduces him to ashes. In another story, the warrior Arthur encounters the 'Cath Palug', which was an offspring of the great sow, Hen Wen (qv). Arthur only kills it after a prolonged struggle. We can therefore conclude that the cat is strong in guardianship, and a good protector of one's own inner powers. It might be invoked when about to enter a confrontational situation, when its fierceness is deemed appropriate. (However, don't use it as an excuse to lose your temper!)

The Otter (Balgair)

A wonderful creature at home in two of the four elemental worlds – water and earth. In Celtic myth it is one of the creatures into which Taliesin transformed himself when he fled from Ceridwen. It is associated with wisdom and the skilful harbouring of essential abilities and inner treasures. It also represents faithfulness and single-mindedness, two aspects well worth cultivating in your journey into other realities. In Irish myth the King of the Otters was invulnerable until killed by the hero Muiredach, who then spotted an otter-skin mantle which protected him in the same way. Thus the otter is a very powerful protector, and when used in healing ceremonies can be a strong aid to recovery.

The Hound/the Dog (Abach)

The hound is known primarily as the animal of the hunt, with its scenting and tracking skills. The near-human instinct of the hound makes it a frequent companion, and almost an extension of certain Celtic heroes. Fionn mac Cumhail, whose hounds Bran and Sgeolainn are of semi-human origin, accompany him on all adventures and are as skilled as any of his human companions. The Hounds of the Underworld appear with white bodies and red ears: these 'Cwm Annwn' accompany Arawn, and they also form the Gabriel Hounds who run with the Wild Hunt of Gwyn ap Nudd, who judges and rides down the guilty. The hero Cuchulainn gains his name 'Hound of Culainn' from overcoming a gigantic hound. Skulls of dogs were used in the divinatory augury of *iombas forosna* (see Chapter 8).

The Bear (Arth): The Badger (Breach)
I have chosen to include the bear here because although it is no longer indigenous to the British Isles it was once familiar throughout most of Europe. I know of no instance in Celtic story in which the bear appears, but it is found in the illuminated manuscripts prepared by Celtic monks. Its strength and stamina, coupled with its hibernatory habits, make it not only a powerful companion but also an excellent guide into the realm of sleep and dreaming. The hero Arthur derived his name from the bear, possibly inheriting it from an earlier god. The god Math also displays bear-like qualities. Perhaps the badger, which is also a hibernatory mammal with many of the attributes of the bear, would serve as a suitable animal today. In the story of Pwyll's wooing of Rhiannon (*Mabinogion*), her former suitor, Gwawl, has the immense power of a bear or badger and can only be overcome by being trapped in Rhiannon's magical and capacious bag, where he is belaboured by Pwyll's men in the game of 'Badger in the Bag'.

The Eel (As-chu)
A great purveyor of wisdom and inspiration in much the same way as the salmon (which it consumes), the eel also has a reputation as a protector. References in Irish myth suggest that certain eels could turn into weapons of great destructiveness when wielded by a warrior. Thus Cuchulainn's famous spear, known as the Gae-Bolga, derives its names from the eel. The Morrighan herself assumes the shape of an eel in a magical combat with Cuchulainn. The eel is an excellent power animal to invoke when defensive help is required.

These are only a handful of the many possible totem beasts or power animals which might be encountered on inner-world journeys or sought out in the world around you. Once you have discovered your own particular helpers you may be sure they will become invaluable co-workers in all your shamanic activities. You may, for example, learn power-songs from them. I have known them to impart the most wonderful and complex songs of this kind, sometimes just tunes, sometimes with words as well, and at least once a collection of unreproduceable sounds, in no known tongue, that reminded me of the claim made by many shamans that they could speak the language of beast and bird. There are other ways in which they can help us discover our hidden depths; some will be dealt with later on in this book, but others you will undoubtedly find for yourself.

EXPERIENCE OF THE ELEMENTS

Shamanism is the most practical spiritual discipline ever devised, with its emphasis on direct methods of working which enable the shaman to effect changes in the environment and on those around him. Much of this is achieved though a powerful association with the elements. The shaman's world is ultimately one of harmony, where the so-called divisions between spirit and flesh, or between human, animal and vegetable, do not exist. This sense of wholeness is also inherent in the Celtic tradition. It enables the shaman not only to move between the inner and outer worlds, but also to cross the non-existent borders within the physical world. This freedom enables him or her to work directly at a deep level on the fundamental rifts in human consciousness, which are the causes of soul-loss and its many accompanying illnesses.

The shaman works with other powerful companions and helpers besides those which take animal form: the elements themselves, which are often represented by power animals or totem beings, possess individual qualities of their own and have much to teach. You have already learned how to work with your totem animals and keep them fresh by dancing; it is also important to dance with the elements. Each is a part of your power; learn to work with them and you will always be in harmony with yourself and your world.

Learning from the Elements

Decide which element you are going to work with (do not take them all at once, but make each one a separate exploration). Prepare yourself by setting up your sacred space and drumming until you feel detached. If you have decided to work with *water*, imagine you are a fish swimming in a lake or river, or in the endless plains of Manannan's ocean. Tell the water all your secrets, your deepest desires, and listen to all it has to tell you. If you decide to explore *fire*, imagine you are sitting beside a fire you have built in the midst of a wild place. Again reveal all your secrets, your fears and hopes, and listen to all it has to say. If you choose *air*, pretend you are a bird, and tell the air your secrets: float upon it and listen to all it has to tell you. When you come to explore the element of *earth* imagine tunnelling into a hillside like a mole, and as you go tell the earth all your innermost thoughts, wishes and desires. Listen to what the mother has to tell you. Listen to all the elements always, tell them your secrets and ask them questions, listening for their answers with your inner senses.

Contact with the elements is of the greatest importance to the practising shaman; he or she derives a great deal of intrinsic power from an intimate relationship with the natural world. The following technique is designed to give you a taste of this; with practice it will be as natural for you to talk and listen to the voices of animals, trees, and rivers, as the voices of human friends.

The Living Tree

For this exercise you will need to find a secluded place, in natural surroundings, where you will not be disturbed. Parkland, or woodland, is especially suitable. Once there, select a tree to which you feel especially attracted, because of its shape, or colour, or blossom. Now go right up to the tree and embrace it. Press your face against its trunk and feel the roughness of the bark. Look up into the branches and notice how the leaves hang from the boughs and twigs. Take off your shoes and socks and sit down with your back against the tree-trunk, close your eyes and feel yourself becoming one with the tree itself. Feel the sap rising in you, and imagine your skin as the rough bark. Be conscious of the wind in your branches, turn your leaves to catch the sun's rays, thrust your roots deep into the earth, feel the currents of the land flowing into and through you. Absorb its languid thoughts, and sense the other trees or nearby vegetation. Sit thus for as long as you wish, until your senses begin to merge with those of the tree, which is a living thing and has perceptions just like you . . . When you have finished, slowly withdraw your consciousness from the tree and return to your normal state of mind. Get up slowly, and thank the tree for allowing you to share its life.

You may repeat this exercise as often as you like. After a time you will begin to get the feel of every tree you approach. Some will be hurt and angered by the things we have done to them, and these are best avoided initially, though one of your tasks later on should be to bring peace and comfort to these beings, just as you would to any human or animal. This will teach you not only a deeper sense of contact with the earth, but also many things which cannot be put into words.

THE TOTEM MOONS

With this knowledge you can now proceed to construct a wheel of the totems, using the same method described in Chapter 2. This time, instead of working with the qualities of the directions, you will be placing upon them the totem beasts or power animals which you have already learned to recognize.

The Wheel of the Totems

Based on the pattern of lunations discussed earlier, you are now able to create a second cycle, this time working with the creatures whose Otherworldly counterparts have begun to be your companions and helpers in both outer and inner worlds. The totem moons are as follows: each one represents not only a creature, but also its inner quality.

> Oct/Nov: Salmon moon
> Nov/Dec: Wolf moon
> Dec/Jan: Eagle moon
> Jan/Feb: Otter moon
> Feb/Mar: Crow moon
> Mar/Apr: Sow moon
> Apr/May: Hawk moon
> May/Jun: Bear moon
> Jun/Jul: Horse moon
> Jul/Aug: Stag moon
> Aug/Sep: Hound moon
> Sep/Oct: Heron moon

This divides the year again into twelve segments, but it should be remembered that true lunations do not conform to such neat divisions. If you look at any calendar showing dates of the full moon, you will see that sometimes there are twelve, sometimes thirteen, lunations in a calendrical year. When such a thirteenth moon occurs, ie when two lunations appear in a given calendrical month, this could be ascribed to your own totem and placed at the centre of the wheel.

With these in mind, begin to set up your sacred circle. When you reach the point where you have marked out the centre and the four cardinal points, place the remaining stones in the positions of the moons. Beginning in the north-west, take a stone to that place, saying, as you set it down:

> This stone I place here to mark the salmon moon.
> May the rising tide of life begin within me here.

Proceed to the second point, saying, as you lay the stone in place:

> This stone I place here to mark the wolf moon.
> May its hunting skills guide me in daily life.

At the next ten points say, in the same way:

> This stone I place here to mark the eagle moon.
> May its keen sight guide me every day of my life.

This stone I place here to mark the otter moon.
May its skilful grace accompany me throughout my life.

This stone I place here to mark the crow moon.
May its knowledge guide me throughout my life.

This stone I place here to mark the sow moon.
May its wisdom remain with me throughout my life.

This stone I place here to mark the hawk moon.
May its swift flight remain with me always.

This stone I place here to mark the bear moon.
May its strength and endurance be always mine.

This stone I place here to mark the hare moon.
May its fleetness be with me at all times.

This stone I place here to mark the stag moon.
May its great heart beat ever within me.

This stone I place here to mark the hound moon.
May its keen senses ever be mine to call upon.

This stone I place here to mark the heron moon.
May its deep magic lead me forever in the Otherworld.

Finally,

May the mystery that lies within myself – the thirteenth moon – shine forth
with the power of [your own totem animal].

With this the circle is complete and should resemble Figure 7.

This gives you an opportunity to work with each of the main totem beasts
and power animals; others can be substituted once you have learned which
ones are most relevant to your work. The ones here have been chosen because
they reflect the turning of the year, and will enable you to call upon their
qualities and skills, in any direction. In this way, you will learn to appreciate
your own innate skills, and have a deeper communion with your totem beast.

You may wish to work with a different being at every month or moon of the
year. Ask them all to show you their world, the seasons and qualities they
represent, and the inner dimension to which they offer particular ingress. In this
way your own understanding of the natural world will be greatly enhanced and
you will be better prepared for your future journeys into the inner realms.

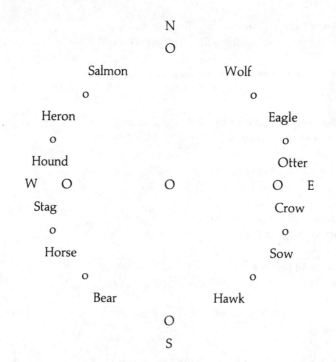

Figure 7. The Wheel of the Totems

Having learned to acknowledge and work with your animal guides, and with their elemental counterparts, it is now time to move forward to the point where you encounter other beings, including the inner shaman, who will become your most important guide and counsellor.

4 Meeting the Bright Ones

How beautiful they are,
The Lordly Ones,
Who dwell in the Hills,
In the Hollow Hills.

The Immortal Hour
Fiona Macleod

MEETING YOUR SHAMANIC TEACHER

THERE ARE TWO CONCEPTS which need to be clearly understood before you proceed further: the 'inner shaman', and the 'shaman within'. These may sound exactly the same, but in fact are very different. The inner shaman is the Otherworldly teacher which you will soon encounter. The shaman within is an inner quality, or aspect of your self, which is activated once you reach a certain point in your training. Once the shaman *within* is given a voice and consciousness, it is he or she who will begin to dialogue with the *inner* shaman, who will in turn continue your training.

Living as we do in a desacralized age, and with only the fragments of a broken tradition to work from, it is rare indeed to be able to meet and study with a working Celtic shaman on a one-to-one basis. Certainly the relationship between author and reader, established through reading and working with the teachings in this book, is not sufficient: because of this, much of your initial training will take place in the Otherworld. Traditionally, the work of shaman and apprentice involves a great deal of travel between this world and that: in this instance you must take the initiative and act as the terminal in this world. The shamanic teacher (with whom you must now make contact) will continue to instigate events which, although you may experience them in the Otherworld, have powerful repercussions in this one.

It is therefore important to establish your own identity at this stage. When all is said and done, who are you? Does your name really mean you? Do you like your name, or have you always wanted to be called by another? The following exercise will help you to sort this out.

Calling to Yourself

Set up your sacred circle and sit or stand in the centre. With eyes closed, chant: 'I am I, I am I', over and over for as long as you can. When you feel that the time is right, open your eyes and go into the four quarters one by one and shout, as loudly as possible, your *real* name, the one by which you have always been called though you might not have known it until now. Let this be your name from now on, whether you get people to call you by it in the outer world, or whether you use it to travel within the realms of the Otherworld. It may be your clan name, or your secret inner name, or your personal totem-name. If you don't feel that you have a totem, then meditate or follow the appropriate exercise first: then, when you have established that your name is the right one (and it may well be the one you were christened – sometimes parents know about these things even if they seem not to!) then go and shout it out.

SOUL WAKING

One of the prime intentions of this book is to awaken the shaman within. He or she is present inside you already, whether you know it or not. He or she can teach you a great deal, and if you follow the teachings of the earth, and learn to listen to the messages of your blood, you will, in time, begin to respond to the wider signals emanating not only from the earth, but from within you, and from the Otherworld. They come from the earth *beneath* the earth, the spirit of which is in us all, as it was in our ancestors – many of whom wait to help us when we are ready.

This is known as 'soul-waking', which helps you to access the deep memories buried within you – the memories of your ancestors, who were wiser, and closer to the earth, than we are ever likely to be. It is the wisdom of the ancestors, the old ones, the grandfathers and grand-mothers – there are many names for but one thing – which we consistently draw upon in all shamanic practice. In becoming a shaman you also become a remembrancer, one who recalls the wise teachings of the past and translates them into ways which are appropriate for today. In a state of trance it is relatively simple to communicate with the ancestors, and we shall return to this subject later; for the present it is more important to recognize the wise self within *you*.

A wholly different being exists within you: not a sub-personality or a psychological entity, but a 'second-dimension' self, or 'second-nature' self, with which we are all born. Most of us never realize this; a few glimpse it briefly and then forget again. To work as a shaman/shamanka you must learn to be in contact with this other self at all times, so that eventually it becomes an expression of your outer self. You are not so much changing yourself, as peeling away successive layers of conditioning to reveal the true self which was established the moment you were born but which, until now, has not had opportunity to express itself.

You must learn to know and recognize this inner self. Very soon now you will make contact with an inner-world shamanic teacher and begin to learn from this source; it is important to acknowledge the presence of the shaman *within you* first, because it is this part of your self who will eventually be dialoguing with the outer shaman. The next exercise should enable you to make contact with that inner shaman, and to recognize him or her as an important and integral part of yourself.

The Hidden Other

Enter your circle and sit in the west, which has the qualities of the emotional and sensitive self. Begin drumming softly, letting the rhythm carry you to the your deepest level. Visualize yourself standing in a place which is special; this might be a favourite sacred site, your own room, perhaps, or even the one you had as a child. It is important that you should feel safe and secure there. Listen for a knock at the door, or see a figure approaching and entering the sacred site. It is you! But not as you are now: rather, as you might be in two or three years' time, when you have completed your first shamanic studies. This is a different you, a more powerful, balanced, thoughtful you. Take note of how you look. Perhaps you are carrying something: it might be a bag, or a staff, or a drum. What are you wearing: a cloak, a broad-brimmed hat, walking boots? Or are you bare-foot? Perhaps none of these things are appropriate, but there will be differences which you will notice at once.

Now try talking to your other self. Ask this inner shaman (who is also you) something about him or her. What do you feel? How do you see? What is different from the present you? Try to engage in a dialogue; it may feel strange at first, but is really quite natural. The inner shaman is there already, and in time will be brought out into the full light of day. By visualizing him or her now, you will have taken the first step towards making that happen.

Ultimately shamanism develops from interior silence and attunement with the natural world. You may see this exemplified by beings of the inner world – totem beasts, power animals, angels, the people of Faerie – but when it comes to the heart of the matter, the essential certainty grows from within.

Make the following vision a prayer or invocation to your own inner senses.

The Vision of the Senses

Come into the circle and in the silence discover who you are ... utter your name aloud, whispering it to the beings of the Otherworld. Once your identity is known, rumour of it spreads through the heart of the worlds and you are known in every place and every time ... Let your name carry with it all your most treasured aspirations: hold nothing back, pour yourself forth in that quiet uttering ... From that moment, wherever you wander, in whatever land, if you sit down in the sacred silence of one of the old power spots of the earth, you will be known, remembered, your call answered ...

Now begin a chant ... drum softly and deeply so that the voice of the drum goes down into the earth and is heard by all who, in the same moment, are drumming also ... Be aware that all things have a voice ... that the earth herself has a voice ... that the trees and the grass and the flowers are speaking to you ... not in words, but in sensations which you realize as feelings and emotions. Understand that you can be at one with them ... Then listen to the voices of the wild: the calling of birds: the barking of dogs and the purring of cats: the bellow of the stag: the whirr of bird wings and the cries of owls and the tapping of woodpeckers and the calls of eagles, magpies and foxes: the whisper of fins in water and the soft explosion of sounds carried in bubbles that rise and burst on the surface of the stream ...

All are one, and all are part of you. When you hear their voices you are listening to part of the song of creation, and to your own voice ... Hear these words ... Whether you believe in a divine creation and a Shaper of all things, or in an accidental configuration of chemicals and gasses, does not matter. The universe and the world are sacred, whether you see them from a human dimension or a divine one ... As long as you acknowledge that, you are already a part of it ... Once you have drunk from that well you will never know thirst again ...

In many ways you are your own teacher. Despite the presence of the inner shaman, who is in many ways a separate entity, there is still much that you can learn from your self. It is very important indeed to be flexible and open to new sensations, and to be spontaneous in all your practice. Be aware of new ways of working; certainly do not follow blindly all of the advice and suggestions given here. Every shaman brings his or her own qualities to their practice, and this personal input is as valuable as any 'formal' training you receive.

THE INNER SHAMAN

It might be said that at this point your *real* training begins: the time when you meet, face to face, your inner teacher. The subject of inner guides is complex and fraught with difficulties. What, after all, is the true nature of these characters with whom we communicate, or who sometimes speak to us whether we want them to or not? Some view them as highly evolved beings, whose sole purpose is to teach us; others have chosen to interpret them as aspects of ourselves. The shamanic view is that they can be both. This is not to avoid the issue; some inner guides are undoubtedly of non-physical origin; others, equally certainly, are not. It may take some time to recognize which is which, but in the end some hard scrutiny and simple commonsense show what is what.

You should also be aware that the advice given by such inner beings is not necessarily appropriate to all humans. Try to find a balance between unquestioning acceptance of the 'voice' you sometimes hear, and a rational understanding (one area where this may serve rather than hinder) or when you are being misled. Once you have established a real and lasting rapport with your guide *you can ask any questions you like*, and you will, generally speaking, receive helpful answers and advice.

The next exercise has, therefore, been devised to set up an encounter with an inner figure who will become your guide and teacher over the months or years to come.

The Inner Shaman

Set up your sacred circle as instructed on page 47. Sit at the centre and begin to breath rhythmically until you are completely relaxed, and all thoughts of your outer life have been banished from your mind. Then, as your consciousness becomes a blank canvas, begin to paint it with images.

See before you a great stone trilithon, constructed from two tall upright monoliths, capped by a third. Above and to either side stretches the night sky, moonless and dark. Between the arch of the stones, however, daylight shows and the golden light of the sun floods out across the stone lintel like light from an open door. Between the two upright stones is your own personal totem, who tells you that it is safe to enter. Go forward without fear and pass between the great stones . . . You carry your shaman's pack in which you will keep all the objects of power you will collect in time.

Now you are in another place. Sunlight floods the circle, though beyond is a night sky filled with stars. At the centre is a table of stone supported on three uprights. You catch another glimpse of your personal totem sitting/standing/hovering above/upon the table. A figure comes towards you from the starry world beyond the circle, dressed in a simple brown robe, with a cloak made from the feathers of many sacred birds, and a cap of heron's feathers. Its face is brown and wrinkled as a nut, though the eyes seem ever young. It may be seen as either male or female.

The figure carries a rolled-up hide, dyed the colour of saffron, which he or she now spreads out upon the stone table. The figure produces from about his or her person five objects, which are laid upon the hide at the positions of the four cardinal points and the centre. These are gifts for you. Look closely at them, then take them up one by one and hold each one over your heart. Then place them in your shaman's pack, wrapping them in pieces of cloth which you will find there. Take care to remember these objects, for they will have great significance for you in the months to come.

Now look directly into the shaman's eyes and ask him or her to gift you with a name. (Alternatively, if you already have an inner or totemic name, you may simply say that you wish to be known by it. In most cases the shaman will accede to this, but if not he or she will explain the reason for giving you a new name.) This will be your inner name (or that of your clan) from now on in all shamanic work (see also 'Calling to Yourself', page 70). If you wish you may now question the shaman further concerning your future training and the work you have already accomplished.

When you are ready, take your leave of the shaman and return by way of the trilithon to the place from which you began the exercise. Then let the image fade slowly, replacing it with your normal consciousness. Try to remember everything you can about this journey: write down the details of the five gifts and the name you have been given, as well as anything else you may have gained from your conversation with the shaman.

The importance of this exercise cannot be over-emphasized. You will be working with this contact a great deal, and the more concrete you can make it the better. Try drawing and painting an image of the man/woman you saw, and make a point of studying this as often as possible. Meditate on the exact meaning of the gifts you received (assuming this is not obvious). They may then be brought into the sacred circle, and will in time become part of your ritual equipment.

From now on you should return to the circle as often as you can, and make a point of meeting with and talking to the shaman. You will glean a great deal of instruction from this contact, and should continue working with it for as long as possible. It may well be that eventually another guide will appear, which will replace the original contact: but the very fact that it was the *first* is important, since this will colour all subsequent experiences.

A Note about the Gifts

You might like to begin collecting these now for future work. They might be almost anything – a bell, stones, shells, scraps of cloth – all possessing a special meaning for you. Some you may already have; others might turn up unexpectedly, perhaps as a gift or spotted in the window of a junk shop. Be sensitive, however, to the kind of things you are collecting – don't go out and lop off a tree-branch, or dig up half the garden looking for a particular stone! Whatever the objects are, they will become increasingly important to you as power-objects which, in time, will be used in your own ceremonies.

A SACRED TRADITION

As stated earlier, shamanism is not a religion: it is a spiritual discipline aimed at opening up your individual potential to the fullest extent, and enabling you to travel in the Otherworldly realms, where you may learn to be a co-worker with the energies of the cosmos. However, while it is more usual for shamans to work with spirit guides and power animals (see Chapter 3), Celtic shamanism is itself an integral part of a tradition which has its roots in the distant past of the British Isles, and which has, at its heart, a pantheon of gods and goddesses, as well as other beings. Many readers of this book may already follow one or other of the deities discussed here; others will want to integrate their shamanic practice into the spirit of a Celtic belief system. This is a very select list of those beings most likely to be encountered as part of your practice of Celtic shamanism. They are drawn from Irish and Welsh traditions, and represent only a handful of the deities you may come across. The positions on the wheel refer to the diagram on p. 82. For further reading see the bibliography at the end of this book.

The Gods

Arawn (Arown')
King of the Underworld of Annwn. A wise, mysterious figure who leads across the land a pack of wild, white hounds, with red-tipped ears, sometimes straying into the world of men. He is a powerful protector, who patrols places which appear unsafe to travellers. He also gives access to ancestral wisdom. Suggested position on the wheel: north.

Arianrhod (Arriann'hrod)
The daughter of the gods Don and Beli, and mistress of the Spiral Tower, a place of initiation within the Otherworld. She is a goddess of destiny and may be visualized as standing on her tower, clad in silvery

robes and holding her token of the silver wheel; she is the primary goddess of the wheel, and also has moon-like symbolism. She is a muse of inspiration and divination and may be invoked as a guide to personal destiny. Suggested position on the wheel: north or centre.

Blodeuwedd (Blod-eye'weth)
Created from flowers by the magicians Gwydion and Math as a wife for the hero Lleu Llaw Gyffes, she was turned into an owl for betraying her husband with Gronw Pebyr. Called into being from the vegetable kingdom she has less sympathy than some with the problems and actions of humanity, yet she can be invoked as a protectress of the wild world and, in her aspect as owl, helps in cases of persecution. She can be visualized as a beautiful Otherworldly woman dressed in a gown of living flowers. Suggested position on the wheel: south-east.

Bran (Brahn)
A titanic lord of the gods, he gave instructions that his head was to be buried beneath the White Hill in London to serve as a protection against invasion. He is a god of inspiration, of boundaries and guardianship, and he may be imagined as a great and noble figure, striding across the land, or as a raven (*bran*). He is a patron of storytellers, and may be invoked as a protector of travellers, and is also a giver of primal and ancestral wisdom. Suggested position on the wheel: south-west.

Brighid (Breeyid)
Goddess of fosterage, learning, inspiration, smithcraft and healing, and one of the most ubiquitous deities in both Britain and Ireland, with many healing wells named for her. Her popularity was such that her attributes and qualities were ascribed to the Christian saint, Brigit of Kildare, in whose guise Brighid still walks. She is a strong protectress and teacher, and her perpetual fires maintain the vitality of the Celtic tradition. She may be invoked under any of the aspects above. Suggested place on the wheel: north-east (fosterer): south (inspiration): west (healing).

Ceridwen (Kerid'wen)
Goddess of barley and pigs, initiatrix of the shaman-poet Taliesin. She brews the cauldron of wisdom and inspiration from which all shamans must one day drink. Visualize her dressed in white, with barley-coloured hair. Invoke when conceiving a new project, or making a medicinal infusion. Suggested place on the wheel: north-west.

Goibnu/Gofannon (Gub'noo/Govann'on)
These are British and Irish smith gods, who hammer out the iron of the soul and the swords of warriors. Imagine them as powerful, stockily built men, wearing leather aprons over their clothes. They are patrons of smiths, craftspeople and metal workers, and can be usefully invoked to help in any manual work, or designs needing skill with hand and eye. Suggested place on the wheel: south-west.

Lugh/Llew (Looch/Hleye) Gods of light and warmth, of sun and inspiration. Lugh, the Irish god, was known as *samildanach* ('the many gifted'), and is still patron of poets and all talented people. He is a warrior, as is his British counterpart Llew, who is also known by the epithet 'skilful hand'. May be envisaged as tall warriors in golden armour with spears of light. Staunch companions in hard places, either of these gods will stand by you through thick and thin. Suggested place on the wheel: south.

Macha (Makk-a)
A battle-goddess of fearsome aspect and great power. She displays little friendship towards humankind, but may be invoked as a powerful ally in time of great need. Visualize as a tall, striking woman clad in red robes and with tawny hair tied back. She sometimes carries a mirror-maze in her hands as a sign of taking the soul beyond life. Suggested place on the wheel: north-east.

Manannan/Manawyddan (Man-ann-awn/Man-ow-with'an)
Irish and Welsh gods of the sea. Restless and skilful and procreative, both carry the gift of sight beyond sight and of wise-skills. See Manannan as a kingly figure in a chariot drawn by four sea-horses: Manawyddan as a druid and craftsman carrying whichever implements are appropriate to the skill invoked. Good for the inception of new projects. Suggested place on the wheel: west.

Rigantona/Rhiannon (Rig-an-ton-a/Hree-ann'on)
The daughter of the Underworld king who was wrongfully accused of killing her child but later vindicated. She is a goddess of horses and of the sacred land, which she guards and in some sense embodies. Her older name is Rigantona, which means 'great queen'. She helps all who have been wrongfully accused, those over-burdened with responsibilities, and women who have suffered miscarriages. See her as a richly clad queen with dark hair, or as a mare-headed goddess with foal at her side. Suggested place on the wheel: centre.

Tigernonos [Teeger-Nonos]
Primal god of the Celts, his name means simply 'great king'. He is seen
as a consort of Rhiannon/Rigantona, and appears in her story as Teyr-
non, a herdsman with supernatural powers and deep wisdom. He is a
strong and reliable companion on the way, and offers earthy and primal
wisdom to those who seek it. May be visualized as a sturdily built man
with dark, close-cropped hair and a wild beard, clad in a sheepskin cloak
and carrying a shepherd's crook. Good to invoke when needing empowerment of all kinds, and for guidance through difficult paths of the
Otherworld. Suggested place on the wheel: centre.

The Lordly Ones/The People of Peace

Essentially these are the dwellers of Faerie, an ancient and undying race
whose origins are lost to us. They are a far cry from the tinselly,
prettified fairies of Victorian times, which many of us still envisage
when we hear the word 'faerie.' Some object to their portrayal as tall and
beautiful people when there are as many references to 'the little dark
people' who were here before the Celts, and who were perhaps the
aboriginal inhabitants of the British Isles. But there is something within
the soul of the land which carries the message of the Celtic blood-line,
and as such the description of the ancient races which seems to evoke
the deepest response within us is of the tall, fair-haired, blue-eyed
champions, dressed for the most part in green, wearing gold at neck and
wrist, and encapsulating a delicate strength. They have a reputation as
flighty folk who, if encountered at all (for they are also rightly shy of
people from our world), are as likely to trick as to treat us well.
Countless folk tales exist of men and women who succeeded in hood-
winking the tricksters, and obtaining three wishes, or gold, or a bright
future. But even here the payment is often harsh. So, if you meet with
the faerie-folk in your inner world travels, treat them with respect – and
remember to be careful in your requests.

The Green Man

Possibly older than all these listed above, we have already met this
figure in one of his guises as the horned guardian seated at the foot of
the Great Tree. He has many other shapes, too, and is most often known
as the Green Man. This figure is so old that no one can really say from
where and when he originated. In Celtic times he appears as the antlered

god who is sometimes called Cernunnos (though this name is no more than an educated guess, based on a partially transcribed inscription).

In learning to work with the powerful energies of the earth you will encounter many such guardians. They exist for a purpose (as do all things in creation), which is to prevent the misuse of the earth; if in recent times they have failed, that is because we have chosen to ignore and neglect them. One of the most important lessons in the early stages of shamanic training is to learn to recognize and acknowledge these guardians. Once you have done so you will find that you benefit in ways you may not expect. The following visualization will introduce you to one of the oldest and most powerful guardians; by following his instructions you will be set upon the road to honouring the sacred earth.

The Green Man

Close your eyes and prepare to go on a journey through time and space to the time before time, when the world was young and very different from now. You stand before the dolman arch, which is carved with ancient, weathered letters, spelling out the names of the gods. Looking between the great pylons you see only mist, swirling and dancing. Then you step through, and at once find yourself at the entrance to a shallow valley. The sun is shining and before you is a rough, well-trodden path which you follow. Rounding a corner you see a palisade of roughly trimmed tree-trunks, with a gate standing open in the middle; a man and a woman are coming towards you, clad in skins, their bodies tattooed with intricate spiralling patterns of blue and red. Their hair is wild and uncombed, their feet bare, their skin tanned and roughened by seasons in the open. They appear grave and friendly as you approach, and speak words of welcome in an ancient tongue which you are somehow able to understand.

They lead you into the stockade, into a village of wattle huts thatched with golden straw. All around are brightly dressed people who smile and wave, or shout greetings to you. All seem happy and carefree in the sun and children play on the hard earth between the huts, laughing and shouting. Your guides lead you to a hut which is larger than the rest, and has a leather curtain across the entrance. On this is painted a symbol which may be familiar to some of you from visits to the Otherworld. The curtain is held aside and you enter . . .

Within all seems dark after the bright sunlight outside, but as your eyes grow accustomed to the change you see that there is a small smoky fire in the centre, and that before it sits a small figure, hunched over something in its lap. In the dimness you cannot tell if it is man or woman, old or young. Each of you may see different things in what follows.

The hut is rather stuffy and the fire begins to smoke, making your eyes water. The air seems heavy and still, and as you stare the outline of the figure seems to grow blurred. Then in the stillness you hear a sound, a muffled drumbeat which grows louder and more insistent . . . For a while you hear nothing but the drum, which soon becomes so much part of your consciousness that you are not quite sure when it stops. Then another sound breaks in: a rattle is shaken . . . The figure across the fire rises. It is taller than you thought and its face is masked in a fantastic tracery of leaves that curl from around the eyes and mouth as though growing naturally. Leaves sprout from the head like hair, curl around the ears and cascade down over the shoulders, becoming a cloak of living green. Two bright, black eyes stare at you, filled with deep awareness.

A voice booms loudly in your ears: 'Who seeks the Green One?' Before you have time to answer the figure is moving, beginning a high-stepping dance to the sounds of rattle and drumbeat. Whirling high in the air, spinning about, stamping and shuffling, the figure continues an ancient dance, the steps of which are as old as time itself . . .

As you listen you begin to feel the rhythm moving inside you, until you can no longer remain still but have to join in the dance . . . The walls of the hut sway around you, heat builds and sweat pours from you, but you are always aware of the dancing figure, who now begins to utter high-pitched calls, in no language that you know, but which the most ancient part of you understands . . . Suddenly you are no longer alone in the hut; the walls seem to expand outwards, the space is filled with jostling forms: animals from the ancient times of this land, bears and wolves, rub shoulders with foxes, badgers and hares . . . all barking and growling or making their own sounds at once . . . And still you dance, unafraid, until with a crackle the fire bursts into bright flame . . . leaping, fantastic shadows dance around you, smoke spirals upward, and you are standing in the midst of a circle of ancient trees, with a starlit sky above you . . .

All at once silence falls, stillness returns to the place . . . and before you stands the tall figure in the robe of living green . . . The mouth amid its nest of leaves is laughing and you cannot help joining in . . . you laugh as though all the world were filled with laughter, with pure joy . . . you laugh until it hurts and you can laugh no more . . . Then you stand still as the Green One raises both arms in a gesture of blessing . . . A storm of wings greets this action, dozens of birds, unseen in the darkness, take flight into the starry sky . . . you try to watch them, but they are gone in a moment . . . only a solitary owl floats across the night sky, its mournful call drifting back . . . As you lower your eyes you see that you are back inside the hut, which has shrunk to its original size. Across the fire sits the huddled figure, head bent over the drum in its lap . . . The beats come softly now, and slowly, like measured footsteps . . . then they fade, and the hut and its occupant recede, and you begin to stir, returning slowly to your own time, awakening from your journey in the place from which you began . . . But in the weeks that follow, you will dream again of this vision, and learn more of the Green One in that ancient place and time.

THE GODS OF THE WHEEL

It is now time to create the third aspect of the Sacred Wheel. Having started with the *qualities* of the directions, and followed by placing the *totem beings* around the wheel of the year, it is now time to invoke the *powers* and *deities* to enter the circle you have prepared. In time you will come to acknowledge and honour your own guardians; for the moment you may wish to follow the suggestions given here. (Please note that once you have learned the various correlations which denote the quarters, cross-quarters, months or lunations, you should no longer divide them up as I have done here. *All* aspects of the Sacred Circle, the wheel, or the cosmos should be borne in mind when creating your working place. They have been split up here purely to make the learning process simpler.)

The Circle of the Gods

When you are ready build your circle as instructed in Chapter 2. This time, as you proceed to each of the cardinal points in turn, make an invocation, either of your own devising or in the following manner:

> In the east I honour Brighid: May she enter by way of the Gate I have opened: May she enter by that path and be present here with me now.

Repeat this formula (or one of your own) at each quarter. In the south invoke Lugh: in the west Manannan: in the north Arianrhod. For the cross-quarters, you may invoke the following deities: in the north-east Macha, in the south-east Blodeuwedd, in the south-west Bran, in the north-west Ceridwen. Finally, return to the centre and say:

> At the centre I invoke Rigantona and Tigernonos, representatives of the earth and the sky, deep lady and lord of the sacred places. That they may come into the circle and be with me at this time.

Return to the centre and meditate upon these figures. Try to see what they look like, ask them questions relating to your shamanic training or your general life situation. When you work regularly with the wheel you will be able to invoke specific deities to aid you in whatever work you are attempting. Those included here are chosen from the chief families of Celtic deity and resonate best with the quarters where they have been positioned. There is much room for flexibility, and you should do as much work as you can on the gods and goddesses for which you have an especial calling. Fig. 8 on p. 82, suggests the placing of various deities from the Celtic pantheon. But these are only suggestions, and should not be considered as either fixed or irrevocable. For fuller details refer to R. J. Stewart's *Celtic Gods, Celtic Goddesses*, as well as to Celtic texts such as *The Mabinogion, The Tain* etc.

There are many other correlatives which can be put on the wheel. Some you must discover for yourself, others will be encountered in the second

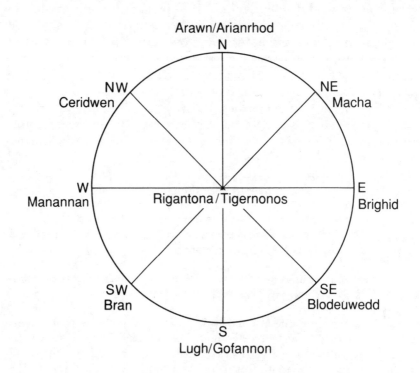

Figure 8. The Gods of the Wheel

part of this book. Before this, however, you must prepare to undertake what will be the first of many journeys into the inner realms; it is now time to put your earlier training into practice, and to discover for yourself the potential of your shamanic abilities.

5 The Great Journey

I will set out on foot,
to the gate I will come,
I will enter the hall,
My song I will sing . . .

Taliesin pen Beirdd

CROSSING THE THRESHOLD

THE ESSENCE OF ALL SHAMANISM lies in visiting the interior worlds, where the truths and realities which abide there can be discovered. From within the Otherworld, the shaman is able to view the outer world with new eyes, to understand things that are impenetrable when looked at with the physical eyes, and to make sense of what is perceived.

All your work so far has been leading to this point. There are twelve stages on the shaman's journey, and some of these you have already begun to traverse. In time you will explore for yourself the many dimensions of the inner world, and make new and exciting maps of your own. For the moment you should follow the schema outlined below.

The twelve stages of the shaman's ladder are:

1. First Realization
2. Opposition
3. Death
4. Awakening
5. Meeting
6. Travelling/Attunement
7. Totems
8. The Inner Shaman
9. The Spirit World

    10.   Acceptance
    11.   Vision
    12.   Second Realization

These stages can be placed around the wheel to show a natural progression through a year of work, one stage being allotted per month. In practice, however, most people will find that some areas of work take longer than others, and I have therefore simplified the stages of the journey into a ladder. This is no ordinary ladder, however; nothing is linear in the Otherworld, and the Shaman's Ladder more closely resembles a spiral staircase. The topmost rung of the ladder is also the first step on a new ladder, which continues winding around the next arc of the spiral, as shown in Fig. 9.
Each arc represents a deepening of awareness: the stages are the same, but are experienced at a different degree of perception and with increased wisdom and understanding. By this route we return to the starting point for this exploration, with the concept of creation as a spiral (rather than a straight line) which ascends and descends simultaneously.

Most of the stages on the first arc of the spiral have been revealed already in this book: the rest are dealt with later. A mythological example, as well as the likely shamanic or spiritual experience to be encountered, is given for each stage. Together they form a chart against which you can measure your progress, and may be summarized as follows:

Stage 1: First Realization

This is the moment when you first decide that you want to follow the shaman's way. This desire may not always reveal itself in an obvious way: you may find yourself drawn more to the outdoors, to the natural world: you may read an account of shamanic practice which sets off a pattern of dreams. Traditionally shamans received their 'call' during a bout of illness, and this may sometimes still occur today. Certain kinds of 'flu have the effect of putting the sufferer into a trance state, and some remarkable insights can arise from this. The call may also sometimes become apparent as a spiritual crisis as well as a physical illness.

The mythological correlative here is of Bran mac Febal, who while sitting in his hall with all his followers around him, saw a beautiful woman enter, carrying a silver branch. With this she summoned him forth to visit the Otherworldly Land of Women, an invitation which

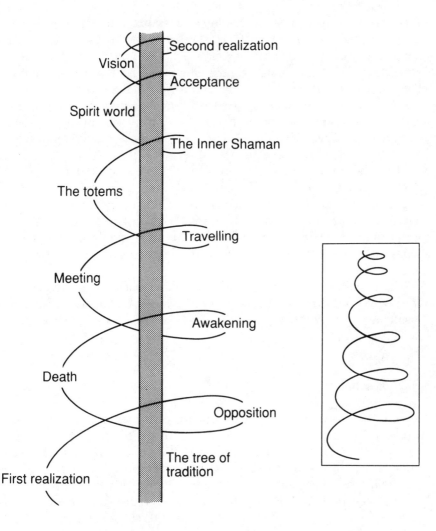

Figure 9. The Shaman's Ladder

sent him forth on an adventure which resulted in many different kinds of revelation.

This stage of realization is accompanied by the enjoyment of inspirational and exploratory shamanic work, where you discover the range of possibilities within you, and when the call of the Otherworld impels you to go forward.

Stage 2: Opposition

From the moment you begin to study shamanic techniques you will find that you encounter inner resistance. The new disciplines of shamanism are not as easy as they may at first seem, and you may find yourself struggling to maintain your original intention. This is partly a result of the various inner pressures which accompany this stage in your training: If there are imbalances or unredeemed aspects within the psyche, the shaman must at some point purge these from his or her system. However, if you persevere and journey methodically and thoughtfully, you will, in time, reach the next stage.

Here the myth concerns the warrior Cynon, one of the heroes of Arthur's court, who heard of a great adventure at a place called 'The Fountain of Barenton'. When he went there, however, he found only an empty basin and instructions to fill it with water, and then to pour the water over an emerald stone. When he did this a terrible storm erupted, followed by the appearance of the fearsome guardian of the place, who drove Cynon away.

The temptation at this stage is to give up your shamanic work, but this is in fact the time to consolidate what you already know by maintaining the rhythms of methodical practice, meditating and journeying regularly.

Stage 3: Death

This is traditionally the moment when the shaman enters the Otherworld state through illness or a near-death experience. More usually today this comes as a result of realizing how futile your life has been until now. Thus you 'die' back to your former self, and accept the possibility of rebirth or transformation. During this time the shaman experienced profound visions and, if spared, returned to life changed forever. In the system outlined in this book this stage has been replaced by the self-questioning exercises in Chapter 1. This does not lessen or invalidate the experience: it merely updates it and makes it relevant for the present time. (A more extreme test appears in Chapter 7.)

There are two myths relevant to this stage. The first tells of the Cauldron of Annwn, once possessed by both Arawn, king of the Underworld, and Bran the Blessed. Those who died and were placed inside this vessel were restored to life, but were unable to speak of what they had seen. The second myth is that of the sickness which came upon Cuchulainn after he had approached two beautiful faerie women. They

struck him with magical switches which put him into a state of suspended life until his charioteer, Leag, visited the Otherworld on his
friend's behalf and eventually succeeded in finding a cure for the
mysterious illness.

The watchwords of your shamanic practice here are: listen to the
voice of the Otherworld, trust, maintain silence. Accept the fallowness
of spirit which often accompanies this stage and understand it as fruitful
ground for future work.

Stage 4: Awakening

Having successfully overcome the opposition and the fears thrown up
by the mundane consciousness in these early stages of training, the
apprentice experiences an awakening of the spiritual centres and a
flowering of inner reality. This is a stage of receptivity, when everything
seems new and wondrous. It is also a time when you should embrace the
vision you have glimpsed with heart and soul and mind.

The mythic correlatives to this stage are to be found in the stories of
Taliesin, Fionn, and Mabon, son of Modron. Taliesin's draught from the
Cauldron of Inspiration caused his awakening, as did Fionn's eating of
the Salmon of Wisdom. Mabon is the youthful god of the Celts who,
after being imprisoned in a mysterious place beneath the earth, is finally
rescued by a band of Arthur's heroes, helped by various totemic animals.

Because of the nature of the previous stage, your awakening may be
accompanied by feelings of caution. Alternatively, this may be a deeply
ecstatic experience. Your best means of approach is to realize that you
are young and strong, and that you need to learn and consolidate. This
stage is best accompanied by the primal work of observation and
correlation: go out into the natural world, listen to its innate wisdom; let
it become your first teacher.

Stage 5: Meeting

It is at this point that the apprentice makes his or her first conscious
encounter with the inner reality of the Otherworld. If, however, you
have already encountered alternative reality, you will find that this
awareness undergoes a quickening as your potential is accessed. This is
when the inhabitants of the Otherworld become aware of you, and
begin to move towards you as you approach them. The meeting takes
place on the borders of the Otherworld and this world.

The myth here is of Pwyll and the Otherworld queen Rhiannon. As he sat one day on the Mound of Wonders, Pwyll saw a beautiful woman ride past. He decided to follow her, but as fast as he rode, she was always the same distance ahead of him. He was unable to overtake her until she waited for him. Like the faerie woman in the story of Bran mac Febal, Rhiannon led Pwyll into an adventure from which he derived not only profit but also great wisdom.

The work of this stage will be affected by the manner of the interchange between you and the inner guide/s who dwell within the Otherworld. New avenues of exploration will open up and your understanding of the intricate links between this world and others will deepen your existing knowledge. This is also when the ancestors may make themselves known to you.

Stage 6: Travelling/Attunement

Now the apprentice shaman begins to move towards an understanding of the wheel and the cosmos. Moving around the wheel of the year new perspectives open out, and future possibilities are glimpsed above the horizon. This is the equivalent of the ritual 'circuit of the land' made by the sacred king and his consort, which not only kept them in touch with what was happening in the land itself, but also at a deeper level helped to strengthen their ability to reign. It is also time for observation and discernment, for experiencing the round of the seasons: a time to collect knowledge which will serve you in good stead later.

The myths here are again ones of quest and search. In the story of 'Culhwch and Olwen' Culhwch wishes to marry Olwen, the daughter of the giant Yspadadden. But the giant sets him thirty-nine impossible tasks which have to be accomplished first. Culhwch is helped by Arthur's heroes and by a gallery of totem beasts, but his quest takes him through a complete range of experiences. In another tale when Cuchulainn goes to woo Emer, she sets him riddle after riddle, and finally demands that he go and become a real man: accordingly, he goes to Alba to be trained by the warrior-woman, Scathach, in order to gain more experience. In each case wisdom is dearly bought, but the prize is considered more than worthy.

Stage 7: The Totems

The first journey is undertaken to meet the guardian of the Great Tree and to gain a personal totem, who will be the shaman's inner companion from here on. Subsequent travels are accompanied by the totem beast, who acts as a guide and counsellor and who helps you access the experiences you have in the Otherworld.

The tradition of the helping animals is common throughout Celtic story; the protagonist, faced with an impossible quest, is aided by a variety of totems. This is exemplified in the finding of Mabon; Culhwch, accompanied by Gwrhyr the Interpreter of Tongues, who speaks the language of all animals, goes to find the lost god. Following the advice of the blackbird, the stag, the owl, the eagle and the salmon, Culhwch and company eventually discover the imprisoned Mabon and help to free him. In literally dozens of folk stories animals like the white hart emerge from the Otherworld to act as guides into the mysterious inner realms.

The work of this stage is usually centred on journeying with the totem; here you learn the ability to seek, find, track, hunt and heal. The totem guides you through unknown realms of the Otherworld with assurance.

Stage 8: The Inner Shaman

The apprentice now goes forward to meet his or her inner shaman, and the realization that the inner guide has always been present is nearly always shocking. This understanding usually results from innerworld promptings, which have a profound effect on the apprentice, although they often appear in mundane disguises. The inner shaman or guide is often stern or masterful because, within shamanic tradition, the teacher is a challenger who stretches your abilities.

Celtic tradition tells us of the experience of Gwydion and Gilfaethwy who attempt to trick their uncle Math into unprovoked war with a rival kingdom, so that Gilfaethwy can rape Goewin, Math's virgin foot-holder. They succeed in their enterprise, but Math gives them a stern punishment which teaches them about the nature of life: he shapeshifts them into various animals, so that each man has the experience of being female and giving birth. Arianrhod is a stern teacher to her son, Llew: she lays a destiny upon him that he will have neither name, arms nor a wife unless he can overcome her power. This is an important lesson, for the teacher always wishes to be surpassed in excellence by the pupil.

The work of this stage will be shaped by your dialogue and relationship with the inner shaman. It usually requires you to balance the inner and outer worlds with greater responsibility, and with special attention to cause and effect.

Stage 9: The Spirit World

With the totem and inner shaman to act as guides, the apprentice now travels with increased confidence in the Otherworld, acquiring one or more power animals and encountering the beings of the inner realms with greater understanding. This is revealed in the use and learning of symbols, gestures and songs which make up the language of the Otherworld. Skilled use of these is of primary importance in any healing work. The apprentice will probably begin to make and collect more items for the crane bag or shamanic pouch, learning to recognize the personally empowering symbols. These objects are like the personal Hallows, emblematic of individual gifts and skills.

The story of Cormac's visit to the Land of Promise shows him being granted insight into the nature of truth and kingship. His encounters with Manannan and the Otherworld show him the realities of his own life: he leaves the Outerworld with the Hallow of the Four-sided Cup of Truth which he is able to use in his own realm as a touchstone of truth.

Stage 10: Acceptance

The confidence which comes of travelling in the spirit world helps you to access your latent abilities, and you begin to draw upon the potential with which you were born. This stage represents the moment when the apprentice shaman achieves his or her first piece of involuntary work, which receives the gift of success and the validation of the innerworld powers. This is often an extraordinary experience, as neighbours, friends and family begin to access your abilities, seeing you as a means of meeting their needs. People will ask you for help which you are now able to give, even though you may feel inadequate or unpractised. Interestingly, this outer confirmation of your inner training does not happen unless you are really able to assist others. You will also find that you will be asked to help the Otherworld and its inhabitants; this is a two-way exchange whereby you thank the Otherworld for the enhanced gifts you have developed at its hands. It is not only a matter of accepting the changes within you, but of being accepted by the innerworld beings with whom you will work from now on.

There are many stories in Celtic tradition concerning the people of skill (the *aes daoine*) being invited to help the inhabitants of the Other-world: human midwives deliver faerie babies, human musicians play at faerie weddings and learn new tunes. Once again the story of Culhwch illustrates this stage well: in order for him to win the hand of Olwen he must achieve certain tests and ordeals. He does so in partnership not only with Arthur and his heroes, but also with the Otherworld itself in the shape of the totems and the god Mabon, who requires mortal aid to be set free so that he, in turn, can help his rescuers.

When you have practised your shamanic skills over a certain period you will begin to have stronger confidence in yourself, despite any initial doubts about your abilities.

Stage 11: Vision

The shaman now experiences the visionary awareness of deity in its many forms, and communes with the goddesses and gods of the Otherworld. This stage brings to fruition the particular and specialist skills which you have. No one shaman is exactly like another: some heal, some divine, some are good at problem-solving etc. Finding your particular skills and developing them is the work of another arc of the spiral ladder. The vision that you receive at this stage acts as the new call to pass onwards. This stage may be spent in learning the ways of divination, augury and dreaming. Divination means 'consulting the gods': it is necessary to go within and meet the gods before proceeding on the journey.

We can deliberately travel to meet the gods, or they can come to us in vision and dream. The god Manannan comes to Kentigerna at night and lies with her as a lover; from their union is born the hero Mongan, half of our world, half of the Other. In the story of Merlin his mother receives a visit from a golden stranger who lies with her to engender the wise child who will grow into the wisest of men. In such communion with the Otherworld, new concepts are given birth.

Stage 12: The Second Realization

This brings the journey for this circuit of the spiral to an end, and the shaman recognizes that this was inevitable from the very beginning. He or she has completed the first circle and prepares to move onward to the second stage, which repeats the first in many ways, but at a higher level of training and with an ever-deepening degree of understanding. This stage of the ladder concerns serious consolidation and assimilation of experience. The shaman enters a period of integration wherein the mundane world and the Otherworld are superimposed in perfect align-ment. To the outside observer, the shaman appears to be a well-balanced, normal individual – this is the final proof that the shamanic unfolding is working. The shaman has a centre of balance from which he or she may mediate harmony and healing.

The conclusion of Maelduin's voyage to the Otherworld very much exemplifies this experience of second realization. He returns from his voyage a changed man; what began as a voyage for vengeance ends as a wise acceptance of the world. Having encountered thirty-three Other-worldly islands, their dangers, challenges and lessons, Maelduin is able to find the healing of forgiveness.

A true shaman is one whose work is so integrated into everyday life that the 'join' does not show; the shamanic practice is unremarkable because it is impeccable. On reaching this stage, the shaman knows that there will never be an end to learning, observation or practice: their maintenance *is* the art of life itself.

All your work so far has been leading towards this stage, and it is now that you should prepare yourself finally to undertake the visionary journey which will carry you into the inner realms, this time to discover the very deepest levels to which you can have access at this point in your training. First you must set up your Sacred Circle and open the gateways through which you will then travel.

GATEWAYS TO OTHER WORLDS

We have looked in some detail at the concept of the wheel of the directions and elements. The following diagram shows how you should begin to work with the innate qualities of the different directions, by perceiving them as pathways leading to experience and knowledge.

Path	Direction	Season/ Festival	Element/ Sense
1. Opening the Way	East	Spring equinox	Air
2. Coming into Being	South	Summer solstice	Fire
3. Passing Within	West	Autumn equinox	Water
4. Finding Wisdom	North	Winter solstice	Earth
5. Inspiration	North-east	Imbolc	Taste/smell
6. Strength	South-east	Beltaine	Feeling
7. Insight	South-west	Lughnasadh	Hearing
8. Cleansing	North-west	Samhain	Sight

A path leads from the centre to each of the eight directions. Each one

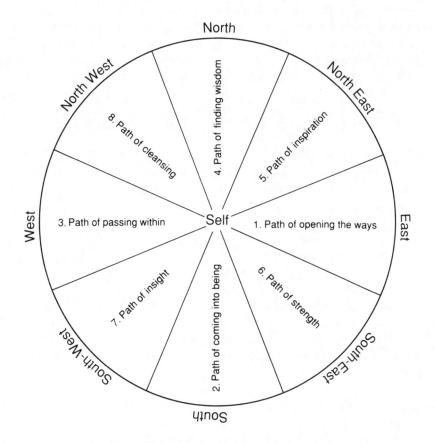

Figure 10. The Eight Paths Between the Worlds

has its unique quality, and you must reach a basic understanding of these before you undertake the Great Journey. The experience of journeying along each pathway and entering the gateways which lie beyond will give you deeper vision. The gifts and qualities of each route follow the informing energy of the year, and are coloured by the directions, the elements and the senses which are our guides in the Middleworld.

You may find other correspondences to add to these, or you may discover your own sets relevant to your needs and location. (Readers in the southern hemisphere should locate their place of winter in the south, nearest the polar ice-cap, and celebrate their festivals and sense their directions accordingly.)

Each pathway can be explored by journeying. This is a way of exploring inner states of being, and of deepening the awareness of the Otherworld. The technique relating to this is discussed on pp. 100–101 below. An open-ended journey suggestion is given with each of the pathways below; please adapt these as necessary when you have worked with them. The brevity of these scenarios should be fleshed out on your journey. You will find that you may travel to the same location many times and experience further revelations and teachings.

1.   *The Path of Opening the Way* is about finding your direction and life purpose, about beginnings, hopes and entering into things for the first time. This is essentially the path of the child who views everything with fresh perspectives. Explore this pathway when you need to find your way, at the beginning of any project.

Itinerary for journey: Sit in the centre of your circle facing east, or lie with your feet towards the east. Start journeying in that direction, using the imagery of springtime and of air to colour your path. You arrive at an island where there is a castle; within is Olwen, Lady of Flowers, sitting in her garden. She is young and beautiful, and understands about the nature of restriction and the need for freedom. Ask her advice about your question: she will rise, so follow her. In every footprint she leaves a trefoil flower. See where she leads you; remember your journey and return.

2.   *The Path of Coming into Being* is about accessing your power and purpose. It is very much a path of finding potential gifts and about the search for self-knowledge. This is the pathway of the young adult who goes on a quest to find the meaning and purpose of life. Explore this pathway when you need to learn a new skill, when trying to find effective means of practice, or when you are facing difficult interviews or opponents.

Itinerary for journey: Journey, facing south, drawing upon the imagery of summer and of heat to colour your pathway. You come at length to a rocky island whereon is Scathach, the warrior-woman who trains potential heroes and heroines. She will challenge you to come ashore and you may wrestle with her and find yourself swiftly upon the ground! Get up and ask her help in training. She has the ability to teach you the salmon-leap, to pass over difficulties with agility and skill, by crossing a narrow bridge which lies before you. When you are proficient you can follow her over the bridge to another part of your training.

3.   *The Path of Passing Within* is about assimilation and understanding, about fulfilment and desire. It is the path of the mature adult who seeks to live responsibly and to bring healing, to find enlightenment and to become more deeply human. Explore this pathway when you need to understand how best to act when problems become overwhelming, when peace is needed, when desires are out of control.

Itinerary for journey: Facing west, journey using the imagery of autumn and water to colour your way. You come to an island full of apple orchards where you encounter Morgen, the queen of Avalon. (She is associated with the Morrighan, but here in Avalon, Morgen is a guardian and healer.) She will invite you to listen to the birds singing at twilight and you may rest in the orchard, taking a healing sleep. Remember the images of your dream and use them to solve your problem. Morgen will help interpret your dream if you ask her.

4.   *The Path of Finding Wisdom* is about accessing the innate supportive knowledge which is in all things. This path is one of acceptance and silence, for true wisdom is not proclaimed by its finder, but cherished and contemplated. This is the path of the elder who has found a measure of acceptance and knows that periods of knowledge are succeeded by periods of forgetfulness or unknowing. Explore this pathway when you are in ignorance or darkness. You may also use it to draw upon the encouragement and support of the ancestors.

Itinerary for journey: Facing north, journey using the imagery of winter and earth to colour your way. You arrive at an island whereon is a feasting hall; within is the head of Bran the Blessed. Any who wish may enter here and listen to him recounting story after story, for he is a great source of traditional wisdom. Sit down before him and listen to his tales; these may supply the help or direction you seek. If Bran ceases to speak, other ancestors may take up the story you need to hear.

5.   *The Path of Inspiration* is about finding true *awen* or inspiration. Its sources vary tremendously: books, films, songs, the beauty of nature, a sense of interconnectedness with creation. When you are stale and lacking in desire explore this pathway to find fresh ecstasy. This is the pathway of the poet who follows the Otherworldly senses of taste and smell to track down the most apposite image, metaphor or word in which to contain the inspiration which flows down this pathway.

Itinerary for journey: Journey facing north-east, using your everyday senses of taste and smell to colour your travels. Come to a cave wherein is Ceridwen, the goddess of the Cauldron. If you ask for a draught from this vessel, beware, for you will never be the same again. She may ask you to serve her in some way in return for this privilege. Drink and follow the images, shapeshifting, if necessary, to keep up with them.

6.   *The Path of Strength* is about confidence and beauty, about self-awareness and the skilful use of personal talents. Strength is very often confused with power or aggression because we experience very few truly strong people in our world. This is the pathway of the warrior who acts as a guardian and defender of freedoms. He follows the Other-worldly sense of feeling, knowing the true balance of the body with the spirit. Explore this pathway when you feel weak or disempowered.

Itinerary for journey: Journey facing south-east, using your everyday sense of feeling to colour your way. You find a dip in the hills and nestling between it the entrance to a forge where Gofannon the smith is working. Go within and ask his help. He will make a weapon, piece of armour or amulet that will give you strength in return for your work in his smithy. Listen to his advice for he is a man of strength.

7.   *The Path of Insight* is concerned with balance, and the ability to make connections and find deeper knowledge; to be receptive and open, the gifts of maturity. This is the pathway of the ruler who balances the realm with insight and compassion. The ruler follows the Otherworldly sense of hearing so as not to miss the promptings which emanate from the land. Explore this path when you need balance, insight or healing; let it lead you to the heart of love.

Itinerary for journey: Facing south-west, journey using your everyday sense of hearing to guide you. You come to the seashore; there take a ship until you come to the entrance of the undersea realm of Manannan, god of the sea and of the Otherworld. Go beneath the waves with ease and come to his hall. Ask for his help: he will set you to search under the sea for the pearl which will bring you back into balance once again. The pearl is tuned to a certain note which you may distinguish as a chant or call. Listen to its wisdom and become attuned once more.

8.   *The Path of Cleansing* is about self-clarification and true sight. The other name for this pathway is the 'first death', and it often serves an important part in the development of the apprentice, cleansing and purifying whenever necessary. This act of reprocessing has to occur in all spiritual experience and it marks the end of one cycle and the beginning of another. This is the pathway of the druid-seer who follows the Otherworld sense of true sight to perceive the heart of all things. Explore this pathway when truth and justice are needed, or when you require purification to undertake a particular kind of work.

Itinerary for journey: Journey facing north-west, using your everyday sense of sight to guide you and colour the pathway. You descend into the Underworld where you discover Arawn in his hall. Before him is his Cauldron of Rebirth: place whatever part of you needs treatment into it, and see what bobs up out of the cauldron in its place. This may appear in symbolic form. Take it forth and place it upon your body, allowing the symbol to pass within you.

Although some of these pathways seem to equate with the different phases of human development, such as the Path of Finding Wisdom which is associated with the elder, they are not intended to be travelled only by people of that age. Older people may well need the experience of the Path of Opening the Ways, just as younger people may benefit from the insights of the Passing Within. Similarly the roles given above can be exemplified by women and men.

Whichever paths you decide to work with first, understand that they are by no means fixed. As you become used to working with the wheel you will find that on some occasions you will feel inspired to change the direction or the attributions of the paths. This is completely in line with shamanic practice, where flexibility to the needs of the moment and the situation should be borne in mind at all times.

When you begin your first journey along one of the paths, it is helpful to envisage an actual road with a gateway at the end of each one. I generally visualize a dolmen arch of the kind shown in Fig. 11, but once again this is not an inflexible rule. You may be happier with an arch of, trees, or a wooden door, or indeed with any image which signifies a point of exit and entry.

This is also useful when getting back from your journey. Although it is perfectly simple to return, slowly and easily, from your visionary state, it can be helpful to have a specific gate to home in upon when coming back from the Otherworld.

Each of the paths leads to a different dimension of the Otherworld, where you will encounter different gods and goddesses, different totems, different beings of every kind. Your entry is subtly enhanced by visualizing the gateway, even by shaping it in the air with your hands. However, remember that such gates are not built by you alone, but with the co-operation of the inner powers, so that a way is opened *between* the dimensions. These are gateways not only to another world, but also to another state of consciousness. Get used to thinking of them as doors to other places and times, where you can walk easily and in the companionship of friends.

Figure 11. The Dolmen Arch

RITUAL POSTURE

A word must also be said at this juncture about ritual posture. For most straightforward visualizations it is sufficient to sit upright on the floor or in a chair, with eyes closed, hands on knees, allowing yourself to become totally relaxed. However, when you come to make longer and deeper journeys such as those discussed below, it is as well to know something of the methods used by shamans in earlier times. But which are still relevant today.

I have written elsewhere (see my book, *Taliesin*) that I believe the squatting figure in the antlered head-dress, portrayed on the Gunderstrup cauldron, to be a portrait of a Celtic shaman and not of the god Cernunnos, as often assumed. The ritual posture is important. The figure

Figure 12. The Shaman's Posture

sits with both legs drawn up, the left foot tucked just under the right thigh, the right foot slightly advanced. Both arms are raised and in the right hand he holds a torc, the ancient symbol of nobility, while in the left he holds the neck of a creature usually assumed to be a serpent – a symbol of great wisdom. In fact, it is possible in the light of other references in Celtic literature that the creature is an eel, which could bring wisdom and inspiration in much the same way as the salmon (which it consumes).

Having used this position as a way of beginning a journey, I can vouch for its effectiveness. There is something curiously free and empowering about it which is somehow reminiscent of the yogic half-lotus position, while being at the same time totally native. For the purpose of the Great Journey an alternative method is outlined here. You may wish to experiment with the shaman's posture, and others of a similar kind, at a later date.

The significance of this posture is reflected by the appearance of the underworld guardian whom we encountered squatting at the foot of the Great Tree when we journeyed to find a totem. This is confirmed by a number of references in Scottish Gaelic literature to Otherworldly women who bear names which contain the word *urlair* ('of the floor'). Many of these were recognized as spae-wives or seeresses, and in each case they would strike the floor three times in order to summon help from the lord of the Underworld. From this we can see that the squatting posture is particularly apposite when either journeying or calling on aid from the Underworld, and that the triple ritual knock on the earth is a very ancient way of triggering response.

The Gunderstrup cauldron also contains several other images of men and women (or indeed of goddesses and gods) in attitudes which can only be seen as hieratic. The importance of such gestures or positions has been established by the anthropologist Felicitas Goodman, dealing with prehistoric, Aboriginal and African examples. Each of the upper-torso figures on the Gunderstrup cauldron reveals a different posture, as the following sketches will show:

INVOKING   BLESSING   PRAISING

Figure 13. Ritual Gesture

PREPARING FOR THE JOURNEY

It is important to do as much preparation as possible before beginning any shamanic work. Setting, dress and equipment – though less import-ant than seriousness of intent – help to prepare the mind for its shift into a new mode of conciousness. Thus, setting up a room in which you are going to journey, putting on clean clothes and any relevant jewellery, and gathering up your shamanic tools (see Chapter 6) are all significant. The lighting of incense is another important process, since this immediately signals that you are preparing to enter a different state of being. Try to establish a regular pattern of preparation, arranging things in the same place and order each time you plan a ceremony, although you should not become too fixed in your routine and every now and then it is a good idea to change this quite deliberately so that you do not become complacent.

You should fast for at least eight hours to prepare yourself for this first journey, drinking only water. Many of the old shamans would have fasted for several days, but this is no longer necessary nor particularly advisable. You need to be strong in body and mind to travel across the divide between the worlds; the idea of fasting is largely a symbolic one to indicate your degree of seriousness.

The same may be said of the lustral bath which should be taken before your journey. Clean, fresh water should be drawn and a few sprigs of birch bark added. Birch, according to the ancient lore of the sacred trees, is indicative of beginnings and cleansing. A single leaf from both the hazel and ash trees, symbolic of inspiration and clarification, may then be added. You could also add herbs or natural essences which have an especial or totemic significance for you.

When you have bathed, and clothed yourself in clean garments, go to your chosen place (which should be a room which can be blacked out entirely, and where you will not be disturbed) and set up your sacred Circle as already described.

You will also need the following items:

1. A blanket.
2. Seven medium-sized stones.
3. A lamp or candle which will not fall over.
4. A helper.

The Great Journey

Clear the room of small furniture as far as possible and set up your circle. In the centre you should have an altar; place the burning lamp upon it. If you have any special power objects these should be assembled on or around the altar. Darken the room completely, except for the altar light.

When you are ready lie on the floor and cover yourself completely with the blanket. Get your helper to weigh this down with the seven stones, placed as shown overleaf.

These stones signify the intent to travel (1); the power of the voice to give

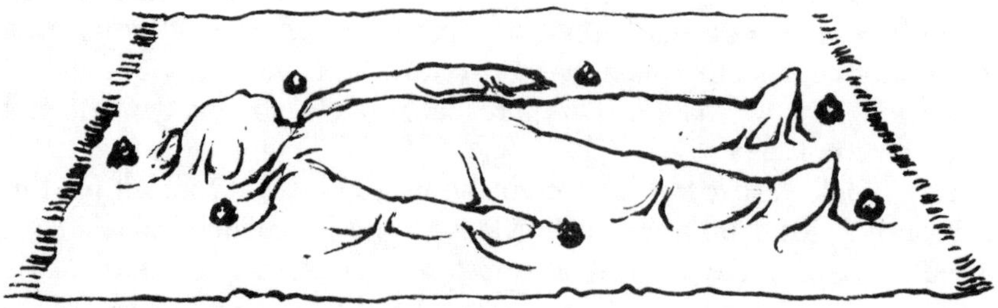

Figure 14. The Visionary Journey

forth the visions which are perceived (2 & 3): the ability of the hands to give the gift of touch to the spirit (4 & 5); and the ability of the feet to journey in the inner realms (6 & 7). The blanket is a sign that although bound into your earthly body, your spirit is still free to travel.

Now get your helper to drum quietly and steadily for a time. Tell him or her to keep this up until you give a pre-arranged signal to stop. It is impossible to say how long you will require for the journey, but remember not to exceed your abilities or strength. These journeys take more energy than you may think, and there will be plenty of opportunity to travel in the years to come. As you listen to the drum, begin to enter into a deep sense of peace and stillness; if you have not already decided which of the eight paths you will take, do so now. Whichever one you choose you should now go forth upon it, following it with as much determination as you can muster. If need be call upon your totem beast to assist you, or ask your inner shaman for guidance. If you encounter anything you are uncertain of do not hesitate to question your helpers, or to make the signal to return.

You should soon become aware of one of the many gateways to the Otherworld. This could be a hawthorn bush, two tall and imposing trees, a stone dolmen arch, or a symbol which has special significance for you. Whatever form it takes you should go forward and pass through this gate. Beyond you are in the Otherworld and all preconceptions should be abandoned. For of one thing you may be sure: the Otherworld is never what you expect it to be, though it may well possess aspects which you will recognize from your study or your dreams. Here you will meet the folk of the Otherworld, beings who will come to you in many forms: animal, bird or fish, as well as in the shapes of the Lordly Ones, the sidhe, the gods and goddesses of the wheel. Some may speak to you, and you may dialogue with them; others will simply pass by as though you were invisible. Try to remember as much as possible of what you see, and keep as still as you can beneath your blanket. The combination of immobility, darkness and drumming sets both mind and spirit free to encounter the Otherworld at many levels.

When you are ready to return, make a previously agreed signal to your helper. He or she should then begin to drum faster and louder to bring you back to normal consciousness. (If you are using a tape of drumming time its length, and if necessary copy it onto a tape with a specific duration.) If the time that has elapsed seems short, do not worry. In your life as a shaman or shamanka you will make this journey many times, and in the Otherworld time does not pass as it does here.

Once you are recovered make a sign to your helper to remove the blanket, and then write down all that you can remember, paying particular attention to images or symbols which may have been shown to you by the Lordly Ones. Later on you may want to paint some of these, either on your shield or drum-head, or on the stones which will become part of your collection of power objects (see Chapter 6).

The importance of this visionary journey cannot be overemphasized. In many instances it will be your first encounter with the beings of the Otherworld, who will become your companions and teachers in the months and years to come. It may also be *their* first meeting with you, and much will depend upon your courage and honesty in facing them now. If you feel that you have nothing to say to them, or are too easily overawed, you will find that they have less respect for you and will be disinclined to help or instruct you when you ask them. At the same time you should, of course, treat them with honour, as befitting beings who live outside the realms of consciousness, time and space. So be sure to approach the whole journey seriously and with dedication, as you would any sacred action. The outcome will affect you for years to come, perhaps for the rest of your life, and is not to be undertaken lightly or without due preparation and understanding.

Once you have mastered the technique of journeying you will want to do more such work, both to improve your shamanic skills and familiarize yourself with the shape of the Otherworld. You do not need to make up scenarios; simply follow the directions given above and travel wherever you are taken. (Alternatively you could use this method to explore the eight-fold path described above). The following is intended as an example of the kind of journey you might undertake, and though it does contain many of the elements we have dealt with in this book, it is not intended to be a substitute for your own journeying.

The Man in the Tree

Prepare yourself as described above. Get someone to drum for you, or put on one of the prescribed drumming tapes. Let your body relax and your senses withdraw from contact with the outer world. Now you see darkness, pierced by a pinprick of light which you move towards . . . The light grows brighter and larger until it forms a hole in the darkness . . .

You pass through it and find yourself in a grove within deep woodland. The trees are familiar but have about them a greater sense of life than you are used to. A stream murmurs to itself as it courses through the glade . . . One tree in particular seems to attract you: a great oak with wide spreading branches and ancient silvery bark . . . in front of it stands a stag of seven tines, which tosses its head as you approach, but shows no fear. You look up into the tree and there, seated in the topmost branches, is a man, dressed in grey with a deerskin cloak around his shoulders. On his right shoulder sits a blackbird, and as you watch the man takes a hazelnut from a bag at his side and cracks it, offering one half of the kernel to the bird while he consumes the other. Now you see that in his left hand he holds a vessel of white bronze from which he takes an apple, which he cuts in half, eating one half himself and tossing the other to the stag at the foot of the tree . . .

Now the man seems to see you for the first time, and without a word takes another nut from his bag and holds it out, miming his question: Would you like to eat of this sacred fruit? Mindful of the prohibition which forbids the eating of food in the Otherworld, and of those who have failed to return from faerie because they ignored this, you hesitate . . . Will you take the fruit which is offered or refuse it? Suddenly there is a rustling in the underbush and your totem beast appears. (If your creature is a bird it will fly down and alight in the tree; if a fish it will surface in the stream which flows through the forest.) You ask of your totem whether it is wise to accept the offering of the man in the tree . . . If the answer is no then you should thank the man in grey for his offer and slowly return to normal consciousness, ending the journey here; if the answer is yes, take the proffered nut and eat it . . .

At once you feel a strange sensation as though you are floating a little way from the ground. You are so light that you are able to spring into the tree with a single bound . . . You seat yourself on the branch next to the man in grey, who solemnly takes an apple from the white bronze vessel and offers it to you . . . Again you are uncertain. The apple is a fruit of sacred knowledge and wisdom: will you eat it or not? Ask your totem if you are unsure, and abide by its word. If the answer is no, then return to your own world having thanked the stranger. If the answer is yes, take the half of apple and eat it . . . At once you feel a lightness of being and a joyful awareness of everything around you. The sky seems more intensely blue, the trees so alive that as their leaves rustle you may catch the sound of their endless song. You turn to look at the man in grey but find that he has vanished . . . You look down and the stag is still there, standing patiently beneath the tree . . .

In a moment you spring down onto the great beast's back and it leaps away with you at top speed, flying through the forest until the trees are merely a blur. You cling to its back and are filled with the exhilaration of flight . . . you feel that you could do anything at this moment, that there is no question you could not answer . . . And, as the stag runs tirelessly through the ancient groves of the Otherworld, you hear a song in the air itself, a song which you are moved to sing also, joining your voice to those of the unseen singers whose music fills the Otherworld for all times . . .

There is no telling for how long the stag continues to run, but at length it slows to a trot and then a walk, though it seems in no way tired by its mighty flight . . . Before you is another clearing, dim and green amid the trees. And there in the centre of the forest is an archaic well, its lip lined with stones on which are carved ancient faces blurred with time. Above the well grows an old hazel, and even as you watch it drops another nut into the water . . . Climbing from the back of the stag you approach the well . . . kneeling above it you look down into its mossy depths . . . The water is clear and you can see right to the bottom . . . There a great salmon swims and, as you watch it, seems to grow larger as it rises towards the surface. Then you feel a sharp nudge in your back. The stag has approached and pushes you forward and down into the well . . . The water is as cold as ice but as you tread water you feel the muscular body of the salmon rising beneath you so that you are lying along its back . . . Then at once it is off, swift as light through the water, swimming down into darkness . . . You are unafraid and able to breath in this water world, but can see little . . . The ride on the salmon's back seems to last only a few moments; then it rises again to the surface and you climb off its back onto the bank of a stream . . .

You look around and find that you are back in the grove from where you started. There is the tree and in it the man in grey still sits, blackbird on shoulder and vessel of bronze in his hand. He waves cheerfully to you and this time you hear him speak . . . (alternatively you may hear the blackbird speak to you, for you have drunk of the water of the Well of Segais and the language of all living things is yours to call upon at will). The message is for you alone and may take the form of a power song or words of advice or counsel . . . Listen well and do not forget what you hear . . .

PAUSE

When you have heard what the man, or the blackbird, has to say, give thanks for your experience. As you watch the man leaps lightly down onto the back of the stag and is away in a flash. As he departs you seem to see for a moment that he too has horns . . . With a last farewell glance around at the forest you begin to return to your usual consciousness, taking with you all the memories of the journey . . . Write down all that you have learned, including anything the man or the blackbird may have said to you.

You can repeat this journey as often as you like. It may not always be the same, but you should allow for this and accept it. If you were turned back at the beginning before you ate of the nut or the apple, try again on another occasion until your totem gives you permission to eat. This journey can reveal a great deal of wisdom and inspiration to you. You could take it when you are in need of advice, of courage, or of power to deal with difficult circumstances. However, it should never be seen as more important than your own journeys.

The inner journey is one of the most rewarding techniques you will learn; use it wisely and you will derive great benefit and knowledge from it. You may journey for any number of reasons: to find the answers to important questions; to help others through healing; to penetrate obscure aspects of lore or teaching; or simply to breath the air of the Otherworld again. Always respect those you meet, even if they seem to play tricks on you sometimes. There are virtually no scenarios from which you cannot derive some benefit, and with your totem or power animals to support you, you will come to no harm.

Not all journeys you take will be scripted like this one. The scripted journeys in this book are intended to direct your initial efforts and reveal some pathways into the Otherworld. With the help of your totemic and shamanic teachers and companions, you will always be led to appropriate answers, resolutions or healing, which will spontaneously arise in your consciousness as you journey. These validations will come with practice if you journey often, maintaining good relationships with your totemic companions and guides. Gradually the Great Journey will merge with your everyday life and inform it of the love and teachings of the Otherworld.

Part 2

PRACTICE

6 Growing from Seeds of Light

I have been a well-filled crane bag ...

The Hostile Confederacy
Taliesin

SEEDS OF LIGHT

THE SHAMANS OF MANY LANDS acknowledge the presence of certain inner human qualities which they call Inner Stars. These correspond to energy centres within the body and the mind, and when properly activated can help you to 'balance' both your physical and spiritual bodies. The elements of our physical make-up were formed amid the cold depths of space long before they coalesced into flesh and bone. Thus the call of space and of the stars is literally within our blood, and when we work with these Inner Stars we are aligning ourselves to the great luminaries far out in the universe. The same is true of the stars from within the earth, better known as crystals. When particular crystals are placed on or near the body, or held in the hand, they resonate with the Inner Stars and can help balance the body's energies.

However, while the shamanic use of crystals has been known about and discussed for many years, there are certain factors to be borne in mind before you consider working with them yourself. A great deal of misinformation on the subject exists at the moment. There are people offering crystal healing, crystal attunement, crystal balancing, even crystal fortune-telling. Some (very few) of these practices are valid; most are at best ineffective and at worst dangerous. You must understand that crystals are extraordinarily powerful, living things. It is inadvisable to wear them around your neck as ornamentation, since they act directly upon the energy field of the body and can damage your health and reduce your energy levels.

Crystals should only be used with a clearly defined intention. If there is any shadow of unbalanced or unredeemed force in your mind the crystal will pick this up and magnify it. They are living beings and should be regarded in the same way as your totem beast or power animal: they must be cared for, and treated with respect. Most shamans prefer to find their own crystals, but if you do not live in an area where they occur naturally, purchasing them is perfectly valid, *provided you make certain that you cleanse them before use*. This can be done quite simply by burying them in salt overnight, or by washing them in a river or stream (or in the sea), or by laving them with the smoke of incense. After this, expose your cystal to the rays of the sun or moon at or near one of the equinoxes to re-energize it.

Crystals have many uses in shamanic work. They are extremely powerful focusing objects, which can strengthen certain kinds of work: healing in particular, or work with the earth. Remember that modern microchip technology runs on the energies of the silicon crystal; crystals are wonderful transmitters. This is certainly the reason why crystals grow on so many of the Megalithic standing stones and sacred circles.

When you first acquire your crystal and have cleansed it, you should keep it with you at all times, preferably within a pouch or in your crane bag. Take it out from time to time and hold it in your hands for just a few minutes so that it gradually becomes attuned to your energy patterns. You will see from this how important it is to observe the procedures discussed here: the crystal can be a powerful ally in your shamanic work, but if handled incorrectly and carelessly it can be dangerous and disempowering.

Figure 15 shows a chart of the human body with crystals positioned at certain points, where they will attune to your own Inner Stars. This will help you to cleanse yourself of toxins naturally, and to induce a healthier balance of mind and body. If you do not possess actual crystals, you can imagine them in place, and activate each one in turn by visualizing it emitting rays of white light. Give special emphasis to any area of the body which you feel requires attention. The object is to bring the body into a state of alignment with its spiritual self and with the greater energies of creation. The Inner Stars are already present within you, and by visualizing them as actively putting forth energies you are giving power to them, and thus empowering yourself.

To help this idea take root in the consciousness, the following exercise may be carried out until you become aware, at least subliminally, of the presence of these inner seeds of light.

Figure 15. The Crystal Body

Crystal Dreaming

Close your eyes. Breathe deeply and visualize drawing in fresh air and exhaling stale, imagine around you a circle of tiny, infinitely bright stars. Feel that you can reach out and touch them. Find in your hands a crystal, then another, then another . . . Place one at your head, one at your throat, one at your heart, one at your navel, one at your genitalia, one at your knees, one at your feet. See them shining there; feel their light emanating through you, melting into a single whole. Your body is ablaze with light; you are emitting a warm, golden glow, filled with energy. Continue breathing deeply and rhythmically for a while, then open your eyes and move around.

After a time you should begin to feel the beneficial effects of such work. However, remember to cleanse the crystals each time you use them. Crystals store information (*vide* the modern microchip computer); if they have been employed in healing work, they need to be cleansed again before re-use. Exposure to uncleansed crystals may result in problems such as loss of energy or volatile emotional outbursts. This could also indicate that there is something out of alignment within you, and that you should not work with crystals any more until you are satisfied that you are well balanced again. If this is the case, cleanse the crystals and put them away in a safe place (always covered in a bag or box) until you are ready to work with them once more.

The Celtic fascination with crystals is revealed by the number of references to them in their mythology; crystal boats, cups, castles, and fountains are frequently encountered by those in search of wisdom or enlightenment. The connection is clearly one of light and (literally) 'enlightenment'. Mannanan, god of the sea, has a crystal boat in which he occasionally ferries mortals to his Otherworldly domain. Merlin retires to a crystal tower from which he views the world. Cormac possesses a four-sided crystal cup of truth which shatters if three lies are told in its presence, and is restored when three truths are told.

The concept of light itself is so powerful in Celtic lore that its importance as an illumination of both the physical and spirit worlds is clear. The wondrous illumination which flooded from Nechtan's Well in Irish myth is both a cleansing and purifying light, which can nevertheless blind those who are unprepared for its brilliance (see also Chapter 8). This re-emphasizes the fact that great care must be taken when working with crystals.

THE CRANE BAG

Our earliest records tell of shamans carrying a bag or pouch containing various objects of special personal significance. Stones, twigs, shells, fossils or bones, for example, are imbued with magical energy, or become symbolic reference points. In Celtic tradition the crane bag has enormous significance in this respect. References to this appear chiefly in the stories about the shamanic warrior-poet Fionn Mac Cumhail, who obtained his father's crane bag by skill and cunning. In the very shamanic tale of his birth and early years he was saved from death by his grandmother, who took the shape of a crane, and who then brought him up concealed from the world in the heart of a great tree.

The origins of the crane bag appear to lie with the sea-god Mannanan mac Lir, who kept certain precious items within it. In a collection of Irish poems known as the *Dunaire Fionn* these are listed as follows:

> The shirt of Mannanan and his knife,
> And Guibne's girdle, altogether:
> A smith's hook from the fierce man:
> Were treasures that the Crane Bag held.
>
> The king of Scotland's shears full sure,
> And the King of Lochlainn's helmet,
> These were in it to be told of,
> And the bones of Asal's swine.

A girdle of the great whale's back
Was in the shapely Crane-Bag:
I tell thee without harm
Used to be carried in it.

Trans. E. MacNeill

These items are all of considerable mythological standing. Manannan's shirt, the knife-like hook belonging to Guibne the smith-god, the King of Scotland's shears, the King of Lochlainn's helmet, the bones of Asal's swine and a bone from the back of the great whale all refer to now forgotten stories, which nonetheless have some clear parallels with the elements. Thus Manannan's shirt may be the sea, the knife of Guibne may refer to fire, the shears to air, and the King of Lochlainn's helmet to earth. The two kings mentioned here may be seen as mythological figures, since both Scotland and Lochlainn (probably Norway) were recognized as aspects of the Otherworld. It has also been suggested (by the mythographer Robert Graves) that the list of objects found in the crane bag are a riddling reference to the five 'extra' letters of the ancient ogham alphabet (see Chapter 8) which were used both in divination and as a method of shamanic communication.

The significance of all this is that the crane bag contains the shaman's tool-kit, with which she or he works as diviner, healer and walker between the worlds. As you proceed with your shamanic training you will undoubtedly acquire various empowered objects which have a special personal meaning, and these can be kept in your own crane bag. All that is required to make one is a piece of hide about 12 inches in diameter, and two leather thongs some 12 to 15 inches long. Make a series of holes around the outside edge of the hide at ½-inch intervals, then thread the leather thongs through the holes and draw up the hide into a pouch, as shown in Figure 16 overleaf.

As time passes you will probably collect a number of objects – stones, pieces of wood, feathers, crystals – which you associate with your innate power. The old shamans believed that such items contained spirit helpers, and seldom travelled anywhere without them. You will collect them gradually through your shamanic work; at certain sites, on certain occasions, you will be attracted to a particular pebble or feather, keep these things in your crane bag until such time (if ever) that you feel you no longer need them; then dispose of them with honour and forethought.

Ritual use sets apart ordinary things. When a stone or twig is placed in the circle, it is no longer just a twig or just a stone; it has become representative of the *element* of that thing. It is difficult for us to realize

MAKE HOLES IN
A PIECE OF HIDE
OR SOFT CLOTH
AND THREAD TWO
THONGS THROUGH
IN OPPOSITE DIRECTIONS

Figure 16. The Crane Bag

this at first; even those experienced in this field tend to see them merely as 'symbolic' references. The truth is that they are much more than that. The symbol has a reality which we can grasp at a certain level; beyond this, we enter a world in which the object takes on a deeper meaning. Once we learn to see the ceremonial objects we collect for our shamanic crane bags in this light, we are operating in the dimension from which all shamanic 'power' originates.

The line quoted at the beginning of this chapter tells that the crane bag may also be seen as representing yourself in some way. Its contents relate the story of your spiritual life. The objects collected and placed within it form a record of what you have done: where you have been, what you saw and felt there. You may include anything you like, no matter how strange or unusual it may seem, but don't try to put in too much. The crane bag is intended to hold your personal artefacts which mark out the physical aspects of your spiritual journey – reminders of the moment you acquired a certain knowledge, or learned a particular lesson. Thus a hazelnut found in a certain place may represent the spiritual nature of the site, the circumstances under which you came to possess the nut, and its symbolic and mythic qualities.

You may consider the contents of your crane bag as equivalent to the Hallows of Celtic tradition. These are sacred and mystical objects which exemplify the energy and resources of the land. Each land has its own Hallows. In Britain there are the Thirteen Treasures, listed in the Welsh *Triads* as:

1. Dyrnwyn (White Hilt), the sword of Rhydderch the Generous.
2. The Hamper of Gwyddno Garanhir.
3. The Horn of Bran.
4. The Chariot of Morgan the Wealthy.
5. The Halter of Clydno Eiddyn.
6. The Knife of Llawfronedd the Horseman.
7. The Cauldron of Dyrnwch the Giant.
8. The Whetstone of Tudwal Tydglyd.
9. The Coat of Padaen Red-Coat.
10 & 11. The Crock and Dish of Rhygenydd the Cleric.
12. The Chessboard of Gwenddolau ap Ceidio.
13. The Mantle of Arthur of Cornwall.

In Ireland there are the Four Treasures of the Tuatha de Danann:

1. The Spear of Lugh.
2. The Sword of Nuada.
3. The Cauldron of the Dagda.
4. The Stone of Fal.

All are sacred objects and subject to quest (try placing them around the wheel and see what qualities they embody!) Together they represent the soul of the land, just as the items collected in your shamanic bag are sacred to you and represent your continuing search for wisdom. They are holy things, not to be shown to all, but to be guarded, preserved and – most important of all – put into operation. The action of the Grail, one of the four Hallows in later Celto-Arthurian tradition, exemplifies this: the Grail is withdrawn from its guardians when they cease to be worthy. It then appears as a vision to other people of integrity, who subsequently go on a quest to find it. In the same way, the objects in your crane bag may become disempowered if you do not respect their intrinsic quality.

Carry your crane bag with you at all times; you never know when you may need it. Like your drum it is a friend and companion on both your inner and outer journeys, as well as an ever-present reminder of your connection with the natural world.

Some shamans also work with other items designed to enhance their skills and abilities. These are by no means essential to the practice of shamanism, but may be found useful at least in the initial stages of training. The following suggestions are therefore offered with a view to giving some idea of the possibilities available. If you feel they are in any way inappropriate to you, ignore them. If, however, you consider that they can help further your progress as a Celtic shaman or shamanka, then simply follow the suggestions outlined below. You may get your own ideas as you proceed, and this is to be encouraged since so much of shamanic practice is of an inspirational, 'inner-guided' kind.

THE SILVER BRANCH

There are many ways of passing between the worlds, some purely visionary, others with a more immediate basis. An example of the latter is the use of the Silver Branch. This is certainly as old as the Celtic peoples, and corresponds to ritual usage among the Siberian and Lapp shamans. It is frequently referred to by ancient Irish poets, who were themselves trained in shamanic practice. It was used both to announce the fact that the poet was about to sing, and as a signal to the inner worlds that the shaman was about to cross over. In modern shamanic practice it can also be used to waken the four quarters before performing a ceremony, or in preparation for a visionary journey of the kind described later.

The branch is simple to make and use. You need a branch which has recently fallen from a tree (you can cut one, but be sure to ask the tree first, and to thank it afterwards). Strip off any remaining bark, and polish the branch with sandpaper until it is smooth, then coat it with silver paint. You then need to attach nine bells to the branch, in any manner you like. Indian bells are small and easy to obtain, but we used hawk bells on our Silver Branch, attached by jesses. These were purchased from the Gloucestershire Hawk Conservency. The bells give a particularly clear and melodious sound, and the jesses, which are used to attach the bells to hunting hawks, are ideal for fastening them to the branch. The finished branch should look something like Figure 17.

I have found that shaking the Silver Branch at each of the four

Figure 17. The Silver Branch

quarters, before honouring them and calling upon their guardians, is a very effective way of announcing your intent to journey. At this stage you should also make a circuit of your sacred circle, shaking the branch as you go. This both strengthens the circle and announces your presence and intent to travel.

DRUMS AND DRUMMING

The use of the drum by shamans in most parts of the world is well attested. It is used, primarily, as a means of altering the consciousness of the shaman, to allow him or her to enter a trance state in which he or she can travel out of this world. Among some peoples who have retained their shamanic tradition the drum is also seen as an extension of the power animal, and is spoken of as being 'ridden', or travelled upon, as a symbolic representation of the animal – usually deer or horse, occasionally bear – from which it was made.

The fact that there is no mention of drumming in Celtic literature is probably because the drum was the instrument of the people. The more 'noble' instrument was the harp, and there are boundless references to this. Techniques such as the use of darkness, or chanting, are discussed in Chapter 8. While these are valuable in their own right, it is still not unreasonable to suppose that some kind of drum was used to assist the

Celtic shaman to reach a trance-state from which he could travel to the inner realms.

The most likely contender for the ancient Celtic drum is the Irish bodhran, (cow-song), a single-headed frame drum made from cow-hide, deer-skin or goat-skin. References to this exist at least as far back as the eighteenth century, and the use of this drum is associated both with Bride's (ie Brighid's) Day (1 Feb), Beltaine (1 May) and St Stephen's Day (26 Dec), on each of which ancient ceremonies are still carried out in the Celtic world. The use of the bodhran on these significant days makes it more than likely that it dates from much earlier times, when the practice of shamanism was still widespread in the West.

Drums of this kind are easy to make and can be obtained in a ready-made form from several suppliers (see the resources list at the end of the book). The drum is resonant and can be beaten with either the hand or a drum stick. The sticks usually supplied with the bodhran, however, are not recommended as these are not suitable for shamanic drumming.

When you get your drum the skin will be untreated and you will need to apply dubbing to help tighten it and prevent it from deteriorating. First, however, you may wish to paint symbolic designs on it, for two reasons: the drum is a magical tool which you will use a great deal in your shamanic practice, and it is also an extension of your shamanic identity. Shamans in many parts of the world, especially Lapland, traditionally paint their drums with a representation of their inner cosmology, and it is a valuable exercise for you to do the same. Once

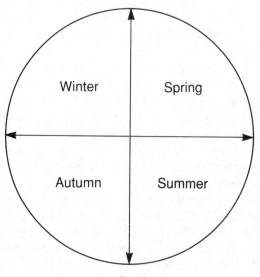

Figure 18. The Shaman's Drum

you have learned to orient yourself in the manner described in Chapter 3, you may wish to paint a representation of the sacred circle and the cardinal points on your drum as a basis for the map of your future travels.

Begin with a simple circle and cross shape as in Figure 18.

This provides four quarters in which you can paint representations of the inner landscape through which you will travel on your journeys, depending on what you experience. You might show one of your power animals, or an inner guide encountered along the way or when working from a particular quarter. Or you may wish to make a pictogram of the kind of landscape through which you have journeyed, noting any significant details along the way. Alternatively you might show one of the four seasons in each quarter, in abstract or representational style. Feel the rhythm of spring, summer, autumn, winter. Can you touch them with your fingers through the skin of the drum?

The example given in Figure 19 is simply a suggestion of what the finished drum might look like; further discussion of the symbolism which might be employed will be found in Chapter 6.

Figure 19. The Symbolic Landscape of the Drum

There are courses run by several organizations to help you to make your own drum (see the resources list at the back of this book). This experience is a valuable one, and enables you to empower your own drum. You might wish to make up a power song or chant which can be silently repeated while you are working on it. An example might be as follows:

> Drum is my voice
> Drum is my friend
> Drum is my guide
> Drum is my helper
> Drum is my summoner
> Drum sends me out
> Drum calls me home
> Drum beats my song
> Drum is my voice . . .

Among most of the primitive peoples of the West the drum represented more than a simple instrument for changing the consciousness. It was also a powerful animal helper, whose skin was used to capture its soul after death. While this may no longer be considered appropriate today, there is still a sense in which the drum becomes a guide and helper within the sacred circle.

When you first acquire the drum you should perform the following 'enlivening ritual', which not only makes it more potent, but also seals it with your personal signature. (The following example is designed to work with a drum made from deer-skin. You should substitute whatever animal is appropriate to your own drum.)

Drum Enlivening

Place the drum at the centre of the circle. Sit to one side of it and sing or chant the power song given above (or one of your own devising). After a time visualize an image of the deer, like a hologram, just above the skin of the drum. Place your hands on either side of the frame and say:

> Fleetness of the deer
> Power of the drum
> Be one, be one, be one.
> Drum be my steed
> Carry me far
> Carry me on your back
> Into other realms
> Fleetness of the deer,
> Power of the drum,
> Be one, be one, be one.

Imagine the deer being absorbed into the skin of the drum; as soon as this has happened beat the drum softly with the flat of the hand seven times. Then take up the drum and cradle it in your arms for a time. This imprints the drum with your own spiritual signature, and allows it to become an extension of your shamanic self.

The drum has many uses; for example, it can serve as a portable altar when placed in the symbolic centre of your sacred circle. But it is used primarily as a means of journeying between the worlds, of setting yourself free of cyclic time so that you may travel in the realms of the Otherworld. Various rhythms can be employed, and generally these will be worked out according to the needs of the individual. There is a saying that 'every drum has its own rhythm', and this is largely true; it may also be said that 'every person has his/her own rhythm'. Once you begin drumming you will find that you slip naturally into certain rhythmic patterns which are your personal 'signature', and therefore the following notes should be used only as a starting point for your own work. It is also worth mentioning here that to get the full benefit from any drumming you should focus on the vibrations and silences which occur *between* the drumbeats – this has the effect of quickly producing the state of consciousness required for inner-world journeying.

As stated earlier, there are three primary levels in the Celtic cosmos: the Underworld, the Middleworld and the Upperworld, all connected by the Great Tree. In working with and travelling to these realms I have found the following patterns of drumming to be especially effective.

Underworld: three beats, very slow and steady.
Middleworld: five beats, steady but slightly quicker than for the Underworld.
Upperworld: seven beats, quite fast but measured in pace.

These rhythms, like any others in music, have varying effects upon those who hear them. I have found that the intention of drumming in a particular range actually assists the passage into the trance-state and the journey into the inner realms. However, you will probably find that your own use of the drum will fall naturally into different patterns.

The drum is a very important part of the shaman's equipment. It is your companion, your soul-friend and your guide; it is *always* your inspiration. So when you sit down with your drum, remember that you are holding something which can give voice to your deepest feelings, accompany you on the most important journeys of your life, and become a friend and spirit-singer in a way that no individual ever could. In time you should develop a considerable rapport with your drum, which will be your companion through many adventures of the spirit.

Always care for your drum as a friend; keep it dubbed and in a dry atmosphere.

SHRINES TO THE INNER WORLDS

One of the primary methods of focusing your shamanic practice is to establish a permanent shrine in your home. Depending on your circumstances, this can be anything from a few sacred objects arranged on a mantelpiece, to a fully fledged altar. Remember to make sure that those with whom you share your space are sympathetic to your plans; I have known powerful disagreements begin with this kind of problem, and it is part of your shamanic responsibility to be aware of others and the importance of personal space.

When such matters have been sorted out, decide what kind of shrine you will build. Remember that this is a personal focus for your work, and need be neither large nor ostentatious. Your drum can provide a simple example, either placed on a small table or hung on the wall. If you decide to attempt something more elaborate, consider what you will put there. Your crane bag may contain objects which are appropriate, or you may seek something else. My own shamanic altar holds some power stones, a bowl in which I can burn incense, some feathers, a piece of bearpaw shale from the late Cretaceous period, a ring bearing the symbol of my personal totem, an ancient North American Indian arrowhead and a spiral nautilus shell. At various other times it has held pieces of driftwood, various crystals, candles, a special cup and a thousand-year-old shaman's rattle from South America.

The important point is that your shrine should represent you in much the same way as the contents of your shamanic crane bag. Shrines are also altars to the gods, and should therefore contain something which reflects your personal dedication. They are not meant to be permanent or static; I have several shrines in my house and these are recreated every now and then, usually at the great festivals or equinoxes when all sorts of changes take place. Shrine-making is a wonderful and uplifting experience which can give you a sense of direction at a time when you most need it. Experiment as much as you like until you arrive at a combination which pleases you. Remember that you can take objects from your shrine, or even the whole shrine, into your sacred circle, where it immediately becomes a focus for power. You can also make elemental shrines depending on your particular inclination: if you want a shrine to earth, make one. Or, if you think that your watery element is weak, create a shrine to water to evoke more of the required quality.

Figure 20. Shields of the Journey

THE SHIELD AND ITS SYMBOLS

The concept of the shield is a familiar one to those who study Amer-indian shamanism. The shield stands both as an inner representational object, which shows the shaman's spiritual place and his or her inner role, and as a sign both to the inner and outer worlds that the shaman is present. Thus the shield of a healer will show symbols of that skill, and similarly the shields of the spiritual warrior, guardian or arbitrator will bear the relevant symbols to portray that particular person's skill. The shield may also show the shaman's name, which in turn often reflects the character and activity of the person who carries it.

The carrying of personal shields is well known among the Celts. These would have displayed the tribal or clan insignia, as well as some device identifying the bearer himself. In both Ireland and Scotland clansmen carried round 'targes' which displayed highly symbolic rep-resentations of their affiliation and prowess. A poem about the hero Fionn mac Cumhail and his band of warriors (known as the Fianna) details their particular banners, many depicting highly symbolic images. This was the beginning of heraldry as we know it today, and though its uses are very different in the shamanic traditions of other countries, it is still a valuable and important aspect of Celtic shamanic practice.

Once you have completed the journeys and the other work described in Chapters 1 to 4, you should possess sufficient symbolic references to be able to decorate your own shield. You may choose to paint it with a symbolic representation of your inner journey, as in the example on p. 123

Alternatively you may wish to represent your particular skill, your totem animal, or a clan symbol. Below are four shields to illustrate different aspects of your training and experience.

If you find this concept difficult, try to answer some of the following questions. How would you depict a hero? A seer? A good mediator? Draw or paint some of your thoughts on paper – they don't have to be masterpieces. There are an infinite number of Celtic symbols and arte-facts to study, and you will most certainly be able to choose something appropriate to yourself. When you are ready, and have found your appropriate symbol, prepare to make this simple shield.

First of all you need to make a hoop. This can be a piece of pliable

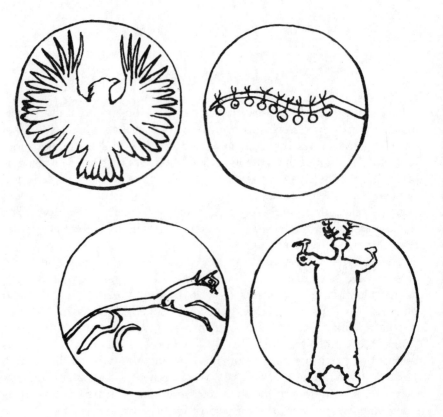

Figure 21. Four Shields of Power

wood bent into a circle by tying it around something like a dustbin or saucepan – anything will do, so long as it is the right size and shape. In fact shields are not necessarily circular; they can be square or oval depending on what you feel is right for you. Once you have made the frame, cut a piece of hide to the required shape and size, allowing an overlap of about three inches all round. Then pierce the edges with holes at regular intervals (as for the crane bag), and pass a length of twine or leather through them, drawing the hide tight over the frame and knotting it securely in place. To make sure of a snug fit dampen the hide thoroughly, and then place it in the sun to dry. The resulting shrinkage will ensure that the hide is taut. It is a good idea to brace the frame by glueing cross-pieces of wood inside, to ensure that the shrinkage does not cause warping. Do not be concerned if you do not achieve a perfect circle the first time round. You may need to make two or three

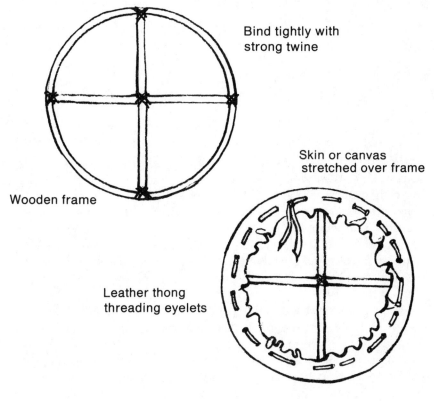

Figure 22. Making a Shield

attempts before you achieve a satisfactory result, but the effort involved is itself important, and invests the finished object with greater energy.

Here is a diagram of how to proceed:

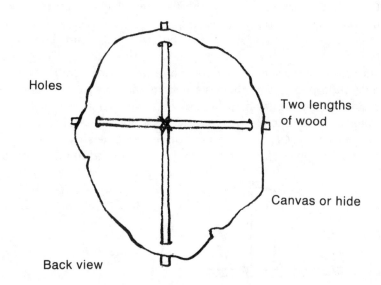

Figure 23. A Simple Shield

There are two variations to this method. The first involves a cross-shaped frame, over which you stretch a piece of canvas which has been cut to the required size. Pierce four holes at the corners to represent the four cardinal directions, and fit the canvas over the frame as already described. Alternatively you might wish to buy a circular embroidery frame, and embroider the canvas with the image you require. Members of the clan which my wife and I have taught and worked with over the past few years have produced some remarkably beautiful and powerful work in this way.

When you are satisfied with your frame, think carefully about what you would like to paint on it. Use waterproof paints, which can be obtained from any good art shop. Meditate upon the design if necessary, and then make some trial sketches. When you are ready, set up your sacred circle and take the shield and paints into it. Paint directly onto the hide, and create a power-song which will enhance what you are doing. Remember that this is a ceremonial object which will represent you in the future at clan gatherings, or in sacred ceremonies you will be called upon to perform.

PAINTED STONES

Traditionally shamans in Australia carry specially decorated stones, called *churingas*. These are invested with all kinds of magical signifi-cance, as well as acting as direction finders and cosmic maps. Evidence that similar stones may have been used by the native people of Scotland recently came to light in the shape of a large number of intricately decorated stones, found at a variety of ancient sites from the Northern Isles to Caithness. Many different symbols were painted on these, and they are thought to have been 'charm-stones', bringing luck to those who possessed them.

I believe that they were used in the same way as the Aboriginal churingas: as both containers for personal power and as symbolic reference points. As such, they form an important part of the modern shaman's tool-kit, and are very easily made.

Select a number of stones with which you are satisfied. They can be taken from a place where you have felt especially empowered, or from a stretch of coast where they are in plentiful supply. Wash them, and then paint directly onto them, using strong waterproof paints. The choice of symbols is very largely up to you, though traditional Celtic devices do exist, and there follows a very brief selection of these. You don't have to use any of these if you do not wish to; they are simply included as a guide. There are many such symbols, and it is important to meditate upon these to find out what they mean to you, and how they could be relevant to contemporary shamanism.

These and other enigmatic patterns carved on stones throughout the Celtic world are thought to date back many thousands of years, to a time before the arrival of the incoming tribes. However, there is no evidence to prove that the Celts did not add to these earlier signs in their own particular way. The Celtic shamans would certainly have recognized the carvings as a symbolic language relating to the seasons, the tides, or sun and moon, and the progress of the individual soul. It seems not unreasonable to suppose that, if they did not already possess such a language, they would have been quick to adopt what they found, and would certainly have developed it. We know that they did so by carving the ogham letters on ancient stones. This will be dealt with in detail in the next chapter, but it is worth noting here that ogham itself has a vast range of symbolic reference.

The stones may have had an even wider application, in what I have called spiritual orientation. As we have seen in Chapter 2, the Celts possessed a complex and sophisticated cosmological system. Finding one's way through this required certain skills we no longer possess – a

WHEEL   LIFE   ENERGY

STARS   OTHERWORLD   GATEWAY

SUN   MOON   EYE   MOUNTAIN

RIVERS   DRUM   COSMOS

Figure 24. Celtic Symbol Stones

kind of inner attunement which enabled the shaman to find his or her way through the landscape which was, itself, a key to the Otherworld. The need to discover certain key points in the land, the power points which enabled the shamans to work their rituals, was, I believe, made possible by the use of stones and carvings. These seemingly random marks found in many parts of the west, may therefore be maps of the soul or of creation in much the same way. A shaman of the older time could look at one of these and *see where he stood* in relation to the rest of creation!

If you decide to make your own symbol stones, you will probably use them in several ways. You may wish simply to carry them in your crane bag as symbols of your particular power and work. They can assist in setting up your sacred circle, thereby empowering it still more; or they may be used for scrying or meditational glyphs, as discussed in Chapter

8. Whatever you do, remember that they, like you, are living things, part of mother earth. Treat them with care and respect, and they will serve you well; toss them away or forget them and they may well steal a part of your power. As in all shamanic matters, it is the intention which focuses the way any such artefact or piece of work is used. Remember always to be clear about your purpose.

THE FEATHERED CLOAK

There is some debate as to the viability of making a shaman's robe. Some hold that it is unnecessary in the present time, and that it simply belongs to earlier shamanic traditions. There is certainly some truth in this, and it must be said at the outset that a true shaman or shamanka is able to work without any ritual paraphernalia. However, it should also be noted that the use and possession of such objects and regalia can be both empowering and helpful in shaping and focusing your shamanic work.

In Celtic literature there are numerous references to shamans wearing cloaks of birds' feathers, and Taliesin, the archetypal Celtic shaman, is depicted on the cover of my earlier book *Taliesin: Shamanism and the Bardic Mysteries in Britain and Ireland* in this way. If you decide to make such a cloak, on no account attempt to collect feathers from an occupied nest. I suggest you obtain a piece of coarse loose-weave material, and cut it to a suitable shape. Then begin adding the feathers in rows or patterns, pushing the stem of each feather through the material and sewing it fast on the inside. The cloak's power would be enhanced considerably if you were to sing or chant a power song as you sew. At the end you will possess a garment which is an extremely potent focus of power; merely putting it on will intensify your abilities.

If you wish to make a less elaborate, cheaper and less time-consuming robe, which can be worn and washed easily, the following pattern is most satisfactory. It requires about 3 metres of cloth, any colour you like, and it is easily put on and taken off for ceremonies. The binding tape for the decoration of hem and sleeves is purely optional.

An alternative garment can be made by sewing horse-brasses onto your robe to create a powerful horse goddess/god dress. Horse-brasses can be found quite easily in antique or second-hand shops. They often contain symbols of considerable significance and energy: stars, crowns, and flowers, as well as various kinds of animal or bird. They can be used as representations of your personal totem or power animal also, and when sewn close enough together make a musical chiming as you move.

Figure 25. The Shaman's Robe

Finally, a shaman's mantle need consist of nothing more than a suitable piece of cloth draped across one shoulder and fastened with a brooch. Replicas of the round brooches or cloak-pins favoured by the Celts have been reproduced by several museums and jewellers over the past few years, so it should be quite easy to find a suitable pin.

The purpose of the 'tools' or artefacts described here is to help focus and enhance abilities which are already present. Thus it is pointless, for example, to make an elaborate shield for yourself if you have no understanding of the symbols you might paint on it. Nor is there any virtue in carrying a set of expensive crystals if you are unaware of their potential qualities. The difference between those who make use of the 'techniques' of shamanism and those who use 'technique' for its own sake is that the former can make contact with the power that informs their work, while the latter can only use 'technology' in an impersonal way. In the following chapters we shall deal with various ways of working with some of the artefacts which you will either make or acquire. As you read on, be sensitive to the meaning *behind* the words, and always remember that the hands, eyes, ears and the rest of the senses are far more important than any robe, painted stone, or drum you may come to own.

7 Healing the Earth and the Self

> The earth — so say the shamans —
> possesses a structure that is related in
> essence to that of the human body.
> Like us, it has breath — the air. Like us,
> it has a heartbeat — the fiery magma.
> Like us, it has a skeletal system — the
> mountains. Like us, it has musculature
> — the hills and forests. It has glands like
> us — its mineral wealth. And it has a
> consciousness, its own thought, of
> which we ourselves are merely one
> aspect.
>
> *Shamanic Healing*
> Marie-Lu Lörier

THE SHAMAN HEALER

AS STATED IN the introductory chapter of this book, healing techniques, which are a very important part of all shamanic practice, are not dealt with in depth here. This is because they require more direct training than can be provided in a book of this kind, and also a longer association with shamanism in general. The exceptions to this are covered in this chapter, and they include, as well as self-healing, the healing of the earth, a far deeper and sometimes more urgent need.

Even as you read these words our world is dying. It has been systematically desacralized and exploited by modern society to the point where huge areas are already wastelands, and the effect is spreading. It is essential that we do something *now* to reverse the process, if not for our own sake then for that of our children and their children. Working shamanically is one way of helping. To the tribal and traditional peoples of the world the whole of creation was holy, they lived in a sacred land, and maintained it by honouring it and by invoking the help of the gods of the land. If we can learn to do the same again, in whatever way we can, we will each contribute to the restoration of the land – and, eventually, if we work hard enough, to the healing of our sick planet.

EARTH HEALING

Earth healing begins wherever you are: in your land, your city, town, village or community, even in your own garden or yard. If you do no more than care for the earth in a window-box you are still helping in one of the greatest enterprises ever undertaken by our species, that of caretakers of the earth. It is our task, literally, to 'take care' of our planet, but in this we fail miserably. The results are all around us: the stinking piles of refuse, the polluted atmosphere, poisoned water, the ragged wounds in the ozone layer, the systematic decimation of the rain forests and much, much more. In a long dialogue which I had with Old Man, he had this to say:

The Shaman's Dream

It's too late to undo what you've done to mother earth, but maybe it's not too late to say sorry and to start over. You can honour her, acknowledge her sacredness, work with her power to help bring about change. If you don't, she won't bear with you much longer. You'll find yourself homeless, tossed away. All the filth and poisons you've put into her will be spewed right back in your faces. You won't like that a bit. I say it's not too late to change. We can begin by building bridges between our two races. You have your ways, we have ours. Sometimes they seem almost the same. Maybe together we can start putting things right, working together to restore the sovereignty of the earth our mother. Yes. The spirit wants that, wants it so bad you may just have to suffer because of it. But if you're prepared, if you don't go any further down the destructive way, you might be able to restore some of the old ways. Let's get up and start rebuilding the old world now. Mother will help us, and so will spirit. Let's do it together, sharing what we have to offer, without thinking: who knows most, who knows best. Let's just share our wisdom-fires and learn all we can . . . Your tradition is not the same as ours – though there are many things that are the same. Your tradition is so broken it's hard to remember. You have to make up new songs. Still, that's no bad thing. We forget too. Our young people don't remember what it feels like to belong to the red face. But there are still those who do remember . . . We have to work together so that both sides of the world can learn to speak the same tongue. We got a lot of work to do, if we are to make things better . . . You ask about the wasting of the land. Well, it's what is happening now and what has happened for so long it's like it had never stopped. You can do something about it if you want. The land is so full of good things. They're the gifts of mother earth. If you look after them and get them spread about then you hold up your head again. You knew this long ago, but that's in the past and you have to live in the present and the future. You have to grow big enough to hold everything there is inside you. Then you let out your breath in one big puff and the goodness is spread all around. Ha, there's no time for thinking: How can I do this, how can I do that? No. You gotta forget about thinking. You gotta act. Use all your skills to see the vision that's there for you to see . . . Then set it all out like a great pattern in the earth. That way everyone gets to see it as well as feel it. The wells are running dry. That's because mother has no more tears. What you gotta do is help the waters flow again. Learn how to breathe in the goodness and breathe out the poison . . . Then things will get better. Hey! Listen!

I have included these words here because they seem to me to put the shaman's view as well or better than anything else I could say. There is much here that we can learn from, much that requires meditation and action. The relationship of the shaman with the earth is all-important; it is the expression of a bond, an exchange of energies between man and earth. In fact, when a shaman or shamanka tells of 'relating to the earth' they are talking of a form of partnership. The earth is whole, a living being in whose complex ecosystem a thousand different kinds of lives exist in harmony. Those who take from the earth must .somehow give back to it. We can draw upon the vast resource of energies beneath our feet at any time of the day or night, but we must always remember to give back what we have taken. We only borrow what we take, and what is given is ours, but not to keep.

The Celts and most of the old tribal peoples shared in this worldview. It is a vision which is as strong as ever in the Otherworld, and which should be firmly held in the hearts of every shaman. When the shaman-poet and warrior Fionn mac Cumhail imbibed knowledge and understanding from consuming part of the Salmon of Wisdom, he at once burst into ecstatic song celebrating the glory of the natural world:

> May: fair-aspected,
> perfect season;
> blackbirds sing
> where the sun glows.

The hardy cuckoo calls
a welcome to noble summer;
ends the bitter storms
that strip the trees of the wood.

Summer cuts the streams;
swift horses seek water;
the heather grows tall;
fair foliage flourishes.

The hawthorn sprouts;
smooth flows the ocean —
Summer causing it to sleep;
Blossom covers the world.

Bees, despite their size,
blossoms reap —
carry honey aplenty on their feet;
cattle range the mountain-side.

Music of the wood is heard,
a melody of perfect peace;
dust blows out of the house,
and mist from the lake-side.

Birds settle in flocks on the land
where a woman walks singing;
in every field is the sound
of bright water rippling.

Fierce ardour of horsemen,
hosts gathering everywhere;
on the pond-side irises
are gilded by the sun.

The true man sings
gladly in the bright day,
sings loudly of May!
fair aspected season!

Celtic poetry and songs are filled with imagery of this kind, displaying a passionate love of nature. The poets — who more often than not were shamans — took on the shape and consciousness of animals, birds or fish in their ecstatic trances, enabling them to communicate, in spiritual language, with the souls of all creatures. In our own time such techniques can help us to see the world more clearly, and to act as protectors against the overwhelming destructive energy of the modern techno-centric world.

I have already spoken at some length about honouring the earth, and the need for the shaman to establish as strong a contact as possible with the earth. The many stories in the mythology of various lands concerning the creation of outstanding features in the landscape, and of the sacredness of place itself, all point to this. They are part of the recognition that the appearance of a place or thing is only a surface concept of reality. In effect a place is made of the sum of its parts: the myths which tell of its creation, the sense of indwelling spirits or guardians, and the presence of people in the land. Thus the myths of the British Isles which describe it as a magical and Otherworldly place, surrounded by the invisible walls of Merlin's enclosure; which tell of the sleeping lord, Arthur or Bran, or the titan Cronos, waiting his country's call, or of the Hollow Hills of Faerie, are all important to us because of the sacred dimension they give to the earth. This in turn projects a sense of responsibility towards earth-keeping, which is as fundamental as our personal approach to the ecological crisis all around us, so that we have to add 'sacred earth' to the concepts of sacred time and sacred space discussed earlier.

When these concepts are applied to the individual shaman's experience they become an outward manifestation of a profound inner fact: that we are related to everything, and everything is related to us. Our bodies are part of the earth as well as of the stars and, like the earth, they are part spirit. When we set out to work towards the healing of the earth we are aligning those two spiritual aspects, our own and our mother's, in a way which enables them to interact. Thus, when we speak of 'healing the earth', we are also determining to heal ourselves.

This is reflected throughout all of nature: we are one with the rest of creation whether we acknowledge it or not. One of the most perfect expressions of this is the image of the spider's web.

The image of the spider's web represents the structure of shamanic society profoundly. The spider produces all its filaments from inside itself, and thus everything leading outward is connected to it. The spiral threads are sticky; those leading to the centre are not. Going out is often hard, returning is simple. But we can always go back to the centre for rest and reassessment. If we apply these images to human organizations – family, clan, race, species – we see how well it represents the way we can all interact, not only with our fellow human beings, but also with the rest of creation. Instead of thinking of ourselves as isolated islands in a sea of other life-forms. We can learn to recognize that 'we' are all related. As the Lakota Indians say at the end of the Sacred Pipe ceremony: ' "We" here means not only human beings, family or clan groups etc, but also species and elements. We are all related to animals, birds, fish and to the materials which go to make up the earth itself. The

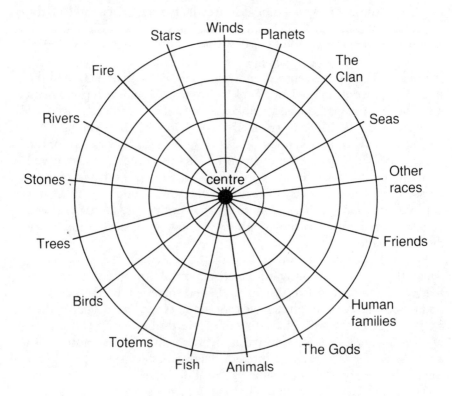

Figure 26. The Web of Creation

very rocks and stones, the trees and flowers, which grow on the earth, are our relations.'

Thus, in the great spider's web of creation we may see ourselves situated at the centres of our own webs, from which the related worlds of animal, bird, fish or tree radiate outwards, all of them *connected to us*. In the same way that the spider can sense when a fly has landed on the web, so we can learn to be sensitive to our own personal webs, to the vibrations which reach us from other life-forms, and to the life rhythms of the mother beneath us.

Everthing has its place, and its relationship to other things, within this order. With a certain amount of effort, over a period of time, it is possible to learn how to sense what these are. Once we are established within that pattern, the aspects of the personality or of the physical body which are out of balance are revealed, and action can be taken to restore them.

SITE WORKING

We have discussed something of the importance of working outdoors at sacred sites, but the time has come to say something more about the reasons and methods of so doing.

The ancient peoples of the world, including the Celts, chose certain sites for their sacred centres because they felt the power of the created earth was stronger there than elsewhere. Such places still exist, still retain that power, and can still be contacted and worked with by those with a genuine reason for doing so. These sites remain outside time to a degree; when we enter them we are at once in 'another place', where we can make a direct connection with the sacred. Sacred space and sacred time are the essence of shamanic work. When you have once worked at a sacred site you can go on to create one of your own anywhere, and with far greater confidence, even if it consists of no more than a small circle of stones, or an invisible circle around you as you stand, sit or walk through life.

Because we are all part of each other, and share a common heritage of blood and life and (sometimes) tradition, we must learn respect for each other just as much as for the world around us. This can actually happen when we choose to work on sacred ground. When we come together as a group, we must put aside the differences and natural animosities which exist in our lives. We are, in effect, entering a region of the Otherworld when we create our sacred circles. The ground within becomes especially holy, and our individual sacredness is there to be respected.

The orientation of the ancient sites was decided by more than simple astrological or astronomical calculation. It was important then, as now, to know where one stood in relation to the rest of creation. When standing within the ancient circles, or one of the great burial mounds, we are present in a sacred precinct where the elements, and our relationship to them, *have already been established*. This is why certain healing ceremonies are best carried out at such sites. Most forms of illness come from being out of alignment with the rest of nature. Within the stone circle or passage grave we are momentarily re-aligned; from this position we can meditate and begin to perceive ways to make us whole.

There is no doubt that some places retain memories of events which occurred there. It is possible, under certain circumstances, to access these, and to learn from them. For example, a visit to any of the ancient Celtic sites, or to places where they worshipped but which they did not necessarily construct, can result in the acquisition of songs, chants, or other forms of instruction.

On a visit some years ago to the Megalithic circle of Brodgar in the Orkneys, I received a chant which I have used often since then. It went as follows:

>Old stone
>old stone
>stone is old
>stone is old,
>old stone
>old stone
>you are always
>old stone
>you are old
>stone old
>old stone
>stone is old
>stone is old
>old stone
>living stone
>old stone
>stone is old.

Whether one regards this as a genuine shamanic song, once sung at that place in the past, is irrelevant; for me it is associated with those stones, and to sing it transports me back there instantly, and reminds me of the nature of these old stone circles.

Once you have become accustomed to working at the ancient sites, and have grasped the idea of the sacred earth, you will begin to need chants and power songs to help raise the energies of each place. The following is one of my own devising, which may help you get started. Once you are familiar with the idea, you will very quickly begin to make your own chants.

Earth Chant

May the earth receive my words
May the earth receive them
May the earth listen to them
May the earth believe them
May the earth respond to them

I ask the earth to hear
I ask the earth to listen
I ask the earth to respond
I ask the earth to bear witness
I ask the earth to bear witness

That her children have not forgotten
That her children have not forgotten
That her children still respond
That her children still can hear
That her children will not forget
That her children are sorry

And I ask the earth to bear witness
That we shall make amends
That we shall restore her
That we shall continue to love her
That we shall continue to love her
That we shall remake what we have unmade
That we shall put back what we have taken
That we shall listen to her voice

May the earth receive my words
May the earth receive them
May the earth listen to them
May the earth believe them
May the earth respond to them . . .

But it is not simply a matter of working at the sites; it is a case of working with the *land* itself, feeling the seasons changing around you, recognizing the thousand-and-one infinitesimal changes that go on in any one place every minute of every day. Your senses can tell you much about these things. Try going into the middle of a field or wood. Stand still. Close your eyes. Turn slowly around. *Feel* the turning year. *See* what is growing, changing around you. *Hear* the birdsong. *Smell* the scents of hedgerow and flower bed, underbush and mire. *Touch* with your senses the sacredness of the seasons. Be aware of all that is happening around you and understand how it is a part of you. This is what Taliesin meant when he wrote:

I praise the god
who infused in my head
soul and reason both;
who, to guard me,
bestowed my seven senses
from fire and earth,
water and air . . .

One is for instinct,
two is for feeling,
three is for speaking,
four is for tasting,
five is for seeing,
six is for hearing,
seven is for smelling . . .

Before you do any work in the land itself, consider the difference between being outside in the open and indoors in an enclosed space. Is one confining and the other empowering? Why do they affect you this way? You may be surprised at what you learn by asking such questions, both about yourself and your relationship with the land.

What follows is a simple earth-healing ceremony, designed to be enacted either at an ancient sacred site or in your own sacred circle at home. It may be performed either by an individual or a small group.

Earth-healing Ceremony

Take your time to get the feel of the place where you have decided to work. if it is a stone circle, walk around it a few times, pausing at each of the four cardinal points. When you feel sufficiently at home there, walk the circle once more and offer a blessing at each the four directions, using a formula of your own, in which you invoke the strength and support of the deities, qualities and powers you have learned to recognize on the Wheel. A suitable formula for adaptation is as follows: I invoke the blessing of the west: May (its powers, qualities and guardians) Dwell within and around me at this time And in this hallowed place.

When you have done this, repeating it at each of the directions, go to the centre of the circle and make a prayer or invocation to the Goddess of the Earth, in whatever form seems most appropriate to you. One such might be: Earth mother, creatrix, preserver and bestower Of all life, hear me and be aware of the thoughts And feelings I offer to you in this sacred and Sanctified place. As I send forth the desires of My spirit, care for them and return them to me, Strengthened by your love and abiding truth.

Having done this, you now need to establish a sacred centre within yourself. Meditate for a time on the plight of the earth, and of the area in which you live or in which you are at this moment. Now go to each of the four quarters in turn, and make a prayer to the land. Let each of these reflect the qualities and correlations of that quarter (see Chapter 2), so that you might, for example, make a prayer to the animal powers in the north, to the mineral kingdom in the east, to the vegetable kingdom in the west, and to the human kingdom in the south.

Now consider all the things that we, as a species, have done to harm the earth in each of the aspects you are invoking. The catalogue may well be a long one, but it is important that you are aware of these things, and equally that you should not feel that you are personally responsible for the entire ecological crisis; you stand here as a representative of the human species, not as its conscience or its scapegoat.

When you have done this, return to the centre and sit down in the shaman's posture (see Chapter 5). Close your eyes and visualize the following:

You are walking in a wilderness where the land is dry and long since dead. Ancient trees that were once in green leaf stand starkly in the midst of cracked mud-flats, their roots exposed to the burning sun. River-beds, where water once ran, are dry and empty. Everywhere are piles of rubbish and there is a smell of death. The sky is dim and clouded: the hot sun burns through a haze of pollution. Nothing except you moves in the landscape, and you feel the sorrow of the place inside you, like a burning heat. Yet you are prompted to keep going, you are searching for something . . . Time passes, how long you cannot say, then on the horizon you catch a glimpse of colour in the midst of the dim landscape. You proceed towards it, and as you draw nearer you see that it is a tiny island of living green in the midst of the dead land. Three ancient trees stand guard over a well, around which has been set a hedge of thorns. There is no break that you can see, no way in to the well-head, from which comes the sound of water splashing. You look around for a sight of someone to help, but there is no one. What will you do? You could turn back at this point, leave the land in the grip of death. But if you do so, how much longer will the well continue to give water? How long before it, too, becomes polluted? There is only one chance: somehow you must break through the thorn hedge and find a way to release the waters into the land. The hedge looks terrifying, the thorns long and cruel. It will take all your courage and shamanic skills to penetrate it . . . Call upon your helping animals or your totem to give you strength – perhaps one of them has a skin that can withstand the thorns? Perhaps one has greater courage than you? When you are ready go forward and push your way through the hedge . . .

PAUSE

Before you even touch it the hedge draws back, parting before you. You enter the enchanted circle of greenness and stand beside the well. Its shadowy depths are choked with leaves and mosses, and where it once overflowed stones have fallen, cutting off the water. You work hard for a time, shifting stones and leaves, pulling up clumps of moss until, at last, with a rush, the water bursts forth and follows its old course into the dry land . . . Now you witness a miracle. As the waters of the spring flood into the dead land, it is as though an artist gets to work with a brush dipped in all the colours of the spectrum. Everywhere foliage returns to the land: the trees unfurl banners of leaves, rivers spring forth again in white foaming showers, flowers spread their carpets across the earth in a thousand varied colours. The sky turns blue and the sun, no longer hot and arid, smiles over the once-dead earth. This is indeed the Many-Coloured Land, a name usually given to the Otherworld – yet this is no faerie realm that you perceive, but our own world, brought back to life by the healing waters so long dammed up.

Make again now the prayer to mother earth with which you began:

> Earth mother, creatrix, preserver and bestower
> Of all life, hear me and be aware of the thoughts
> And feelings I offer to you in this sacred and
> Sanctified place. As I send forth the desires of
> My spirit, care for them and return them to me,
> Strengthened by your love and abiding truth.

When you are ready, return fully to your normal consciousness and thank your power animals or totem for their help. Then go to each of the quarters and thank the powers and elements who supported you in this work, before dismantling your circle or departing from the site in which you have worked.

You may perform this ceremony as often as you wish. Indeed, you should practise it as often as possible, and with as many people as you can. It is a way of re-energizing the earth, and of reminding our mother that we have not forgotten her plight.

HEALING OTHERS

In essence the shaman seeks to heal the soul, rather than the body, of the individual, though he may work on both if the nature of the sickness requires it. Most cures are achieved through ecstatic trance, in which the shaman journeys to the inner worlds, from where he or she can work directly on the illness, which is perceived in a wholly different manner from such a vantage-point. Thus, healing ceremonies such as the sand-paintings of the Navajo work on the assumption of an inner-relatedness with all things. The sand painter creates representations of the spirits who are connected with various parts of the body, and touches the affected part with sand from the picture. This is more than a symbolic representation; it is in a sense the *bringing-through* of the Otherworld into this world, or into the sacred space which is between, but touching both worlds. Different laws operate in the Otherworld, and if the circle has been properly set up the shaman will be able to operate within it according to those very different laws.

The following is one of the safer and simpler methods of healing yourself and others, and may be practised with care and with the agreement of those involved.

'The hands of the shaman are the hands of a healer.' So I was told by my own inner shaman, and so I have always believed. Once you have discovered your power animal (or animals), and your inner shamanic guide, and once you have learned some power songs or chants of your own, it is perfectly possible to practise this kind of healing yourself. However, *you should only do so when you are certain you have reached a stage of shamanic proficiency* – for example, when you have completed at least a year's work based on this book or an alternative teaching method – as to do otherwise could harm both you and your patient. Always remember that these techniques are not a substitute for general medical care. They can be both an adjunct and a supporter, and they can help in rebalancing the patient who has suffered poor health for a long period.

The Healing Gift

Begin by setting up your sacred circle. Invite your patient into the circle and ask him or her to lie down. If you are using incense, gently blow a little smoke over the patient. Now establish the area of the body which is causing the trouble (but not the exact symptoms – this merely confuses your direct sight). You should have with you a stone, or piece of wood, which you have previously requested permission to use as a receiver of the sickness. Hold it for a time while you use your inner senses and vision to seek out the root of the problem. When you feel that you know what is wrong – this may appear as an inner vision of a particular colour, a shadow on the aura of the patient, or even as a shape – put down the stone/stick and hold your hand slightly above the affected part with the middle finger and the thumb pointing downwards (See Figure 27).

Begin chanting a power song, which might be something like the following:

> Healing come
> Healing come
> Healing found
> Healing bound
> Healing sound
> Healing round
> Healing come
> Healing done etc.

Keep this up until you enter a light trance state and feel the negative energy of the patient rise to the surface. An intensification of the colour, or deepening of

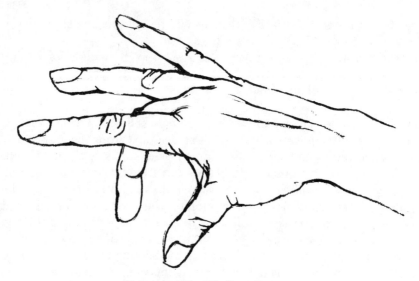

Figure 27. The Healing Gesture

the shadow, will tell you when this occurs, and you should also feel a tingling in your hands. When you are ready, touch the patient lightly on the area affected with your thumb and middle finger, and transfer the negative energy to the stone or stick. This is done by offering a prayer to the goddess of the earth to make you a vehicle for the transference. Now, as quickly as possible, break the trance state, tell the patient to remain in the circle and at once remove the stone/stick to a safe distance, chanting your power song all the while. Take care how you handle the object and cleanse it as soon as you can, either by burying it in the earth or by holding it beneath running water (preferably a stream, but tap-water will serve at need). Return to the patient and help him/her to stand; lead him/her out of the circle and thank the powers which have assisted you. Next dismantle the circle, and earth yourself by eating or drinking. At least one hour later reclaim the stone or stick from where you placed it, and return it to its natural environment. Never use the same object more than once for this kind of healing. The earth/water will carry away all infection or negative energy in a matter of hours.

Such techniques are very ancient, and have been tried and tested on willing subjects with varied success. I have found that with a little practice it is possible to see a manifestation of the ailment as an almost physical thing. On one occasion when I was working on a subject with an internal complaint I actually saw a white worm coiled up inside. In this instance I visualized sending a red worm into the patient to drive out the other, whilst chanting vigorously to 'tell' the negative creature that I was there. I sang and chanted and drummed for some time after until I was certain the negative energy was less strong and active. Nonetheless the patient continued to suffer for several days after, eventually making a good recovery.

INCUBATION AND DREAMS

Another method of healing practised among the Celts (as in many other parts of the ancient world) was that of incubation. Here the sufferer, after being suitably prepared, slept in a special hut or cave, and there incubated a dream in which he or she either received a visitation from one of the gods of healing, or was instructed in a method of self-cure – often cryptically, and in a form requiring interpretation.

Our ancestors possessed the ability to dream truths they were unaware of in their outer lives. We have largely lost this ability today, and when we do dream the images and ideas we receive are often incoherent and fragmented. We have thus to learn over again not only how to dream and to remember what we dream, but to be in touch with our dreaming so that we are able to 'dream true'.

The early shamans saw sickness as a reflection of spiritual health, and therefore if a person suffered from a physical ailment (excluding loss of limbs or wounds acquired in war) this meant that there must be something wrong with his soul. Incubatory sleep thus became the shaman's principal method of working his cures – much as in modern psychoanalytical treatment, where the patient is encouraged to discover the disaffection in his or her soul through the study or interpretation of his dreams.

Unlike modern psychological practice, however, the dreams were seen as specifically emanating from deity, and the whole process took place within a specific *temenos*, a sacred precinct dedicated to one or other of the gods associated with healing. The resultant dreams (and few seem not to have experienced something) either effected an immediate cure, or gave a method by which this might be achieved.

Preparation for the ritual of dreaming was also carefully controlled. After undergoing rites of purification, involving a lustral bath and offerings to the god, the sufferer went to sleep in the place prepared, assured of privacy. The importance of this routine is stressed in every account of incubation temples; if the patients were not in a proper state of mind, they were likely either not to experience a dream or to have one which was unsatisfactory. Those who did so were usually sent away, perhaps to try again later, after a further period of preparation. Patients at the incubation temples who failed to sleep at all (either from excitement or pain), apparently received a direct vision of the god, in which they were instructed as to how they might achieve healing, in the same way as if they had experienced a dream.

It is also clear that the incubatory sleep took place at night, which is relevant when one considers the stress laid upon the absence of light by the Celtic shaman-poets and prophets, who frequently gave forth their precognitive visions when, after being enclosed in a dark place, they were brought forth into bright light (see Chapter 8).

That some form of incubatory sleep was practised among the Celts is well attested, and various stories make oblique reference to incubation. In the Irish story of 'The Sickbed of Cuchulainn', for instance, the hero is afflicted with a strange wasting sickness from which he is later cured after falling asleep and dreaming of the Otherworld. There is also a suggestion in the story that the sickness *originated* in the Otherworld, which accords well with the shamanic idea that all illness is of an ultimately spiritual origin. Certainly the prime cause of sickness was seen as emanating from the presence of an unfriendly spirit, which caused the sufferer to be out of alignment with the rest of creation. It is more than likely that stories of this kind are the product of a distant memory of incubatory methods which included a visionary journey to the Otherworld in search of a cure (see p. 147–9 for an example of this kind of work).

Elsewhere in Celtic literature we learn of the existence of *teach-an-alais* (sweat-houses) which, though they were used primarily for healing, may well have been utilized for the kind of cleansing journey practised among the Amerindian peoples in their sweat lodges. The Irish sweat-houses were roughly beehive-shaped, and had a low entrance. Fires were lit inside, and when the floor and walls were suitably hot, the ashes were raked out and turf sods placed within. The combination of heat and the moist turfs created a steamy atmosphere in which the sufferer was then laid. The doorway was then closed, and the patient was left alone for a time.

The similarity between this practice and that of dream incubation (as well as the inspirational oriented work to be discussed in the next chapter) is remarkable. Further evidence comes from excavations carried out some years ago at the site of a Romano-British temple at Lydney in Gloucestershire. This was found to possess a striking resemblance to ancient *abatons* (sleep-temples) excavated in Greece, and the noted archaeologist Sir Mortimer Wheeler, who carried out the excavations, thought there was a strong possibility of the site being created for the same purpose. The site was dedicated to the god Nodens, who shared something of the attributes of the Greek healer-god Asklepios. As with most Celtic deities we have no representation of Nodens, but evidence suggests that he was a bright figure who radiated light, and that he was accompanied by a dog. Further evidence of this is found in several Irish and Welsh texts, where Nodens' cognates are Nuada and Gwynn ap Nudd, both of whom are associated with water, light and dogs.

Today a number of people are working with the idea of incubatory sleep as a method of healing and/or learning. I have led several such groups, and the following notes are based in part on the experience of these workshops.

The Dream

Find a space where you will be undisturbed for at least an hour. Then set up your circle in the prescribed manner and reduce the light to that of a single candle placed on a central table or altar. Do not perform this exercise late at night when you are tired, and about to retire for the night. The dream you are seeking should come to you while you are sufficiently alert to be aware of its content, which you will almost certainly need to record afterwards.

Spend a little time in quiet, preparing yourself for the vision you hope to be granted. The emphasis placed on preparation in the ancient healing temples was of great importance – if you are feeling upset, angry, or distracted you will be less likely to receive a healing dream.

When you feel sufficiently prepared, light some incense and read aloud the following invocation:

> Learn to be gifted with the night,
> With the words of wisdom.
> From the depths of darkness' dazzling
> The story will rise
> As a circling snake.
>
> May the sacred curve of her arm enfold you!
> May the stars of Her dark veil cover you!
> May your sleep be founded
> In the deep night of Her own lap!

Now begin to study the diagram printed overleaf (Fig. 28) until it is sufficiently imprinted on your mind that you can close your eyes and still 'see' it.

Lie down flat on your back on the floor, with feet together, and compose yourself as if for sleep. This position is the result of much practice; lying on the side promotes deep sleep and less ease of communication with the dream state. Keep the image of the spiral maze in your mind as you do so – it is an image of great potency, and will assist you in making the passage from normal consciousness to the incubatory state.

After a while begin to zero in upon the centre of the maze, and see that there

Figure 28. The Spiral Maze

is a small door set there. As you look it grows larger, until it is big enough to pass through. As you approach the door opens and a figure comes forth to welcome you. This may take the form of a man or woman, or possibly even your usual inner shamanic guide. Either way he or she will welcome you, and lead you through the door at the heart of the maze and into a large, roomy cave, lit by torches, with a number of smaller rooms leading off from it. Your guide offers you a drink of clear, cold water, before taking you to one of these. You find a small cot made up for you; when you lie upon it, it is remarkably comfortable. When your guide is assured that you are settled you are left alone. The room is dark save for the reflections of torchlight from the main chamber. You drift off to sleep watching the dancing shadows in the cave beyond . . .

What happens next depends on a number of factors. If you have prepared yourself properly you should experience either a dream or a waking vision, in which you will be told the best way to cure yourself (or, if you are doing this for another, him or her). The answer may come in the form of a visit from the god Nodens, perhaps accompanied by one of his sacred dogs, a lick from whose tongue itself brings healing. Or it may be that you will see someone whom you may have met during a visionary journey or meditation. Alternatively, you may be shown a scene, a single image, or number of images, which may mean nothing at all to you. If this is the case make certain that you remember these and record them as faithfully as possible when you wake up. You may need to meditate upon them several times before they yield up their meaning, but you may be sure that they will contain a message concerning the healing.

When you are certain that you have a sufficiently clear grasp of what you have been shown or told, begin to wake yourself up. This is not as difficult as it sounds. You will find, perhaps after a few attempts, that you are able to bring yourself back to a state of full awareness quite easily. Take your time, however, or you may experience a certain degree of disorientation.

If you do not receive a dream, do not worry. It may take a little time to accustom yourself to what is essentially a slightly different kind of sleep from normal. I have known dreamers to get nothing at all in their first session, and then to have an extraordinarily relevant dream on the following night in a perfectly usual way. Others have had to make the journey to the cave several times before they receive the message they are seeking. You can be sure that, sooner or later, you will get a significant dream from this exercise and that it will contain the necessary information to accomplish a healing state.

SOUL-RETRIEVAL

One of the least understood aspects of shamanic work is soul-retrieval, in which the shaman journeys to retrieve the soul of a sick person, who may be near to death. It relates closely to the underlying theme of this book, the phenomenon of 'soul-loss' experienced by so many people today. If the dedication of the shaman is, as I believe, to confront and combat this increasingly common problem, then some practice of the kind described here is ultimately of considerable importance (see *Soul Retrieval* by Sandra Ingerman).

Some time ago a member of my wife's family became suddenly and inexplicably ill. Hospitalized, she seemed to have given up all desire to live and was slowly, but steadily, fading. The hospital was too far away for me to visit her, so I decided to attempt a soul-retrieval from afar. I sat in the centre of my circle and drummed for a long time until I felt very deeply entranced. Then, calling upon my personal power animal to help me, I visualized the face of the sick person, and projected my inner body out in search of her. What happened next is difficult to describe. I felt myself floating in a dark, timeless place, where there were no physical feelings at all. Yet I was aware that I was somehow moving – though how swiftly or slowly I could not say – and in the distance I began to discern a greyish glimmer of light. As it drew nearer – or as I approached it – I saw that it was a face, the face of the person I was seeking. It floated, as did I, in a place that seemed like nowhere – and then it retreated from me, going further away. I exerted all my will and projected a silent shout – the person's name. There was no immediate response, but I continued to repeat the name as if it were a chant. At length I saw the 'face' move closer to me, and felt that it was aware of my presence. I asked if it knew where it was, or what was happening to its body. It seemed to be confused. I sent out as strong a message as I could to say that, if the time was not yet right for the spirit to pass onward to its next stage of development, it should return to its body. Slowly, the face faded and I began my own journey back. I was very tired when I returned, but that night heard that the patient had begun to show signs of alertness and to ask for water, simultaneously with my soul-retrieval.

There is no exact method for this kind of work. I simply set up my circle, called on my power animals to support me, drummed myself into a trance state and went forth. I have no idea 'how' I did this; it is simply a technique which the practising shaman develops after a while. I have repeated the exercise several times, and have felt no ill-effects. I have been asked whether there was any danger of 'getting stuck' in the 'nowhere' place, which is a kind of limbo for spirits. Some practitioners recommend extreme caution here, but I truly believe that there is no danger so long as (as in any shamanic journey) you go with clear intentions and take your power animals. If you wish to attempt this exercise and feel nervous of the outcome, get someone to drum for you and agree on a sign by which he or she will know that you wish to be drummed back up.

It is also important to understand that you, as the shaman attempting this technique, are *not* the one who decides whether the patient will live or die. If their allotted time is over it is wrong to interfere. Always remember to ask the wandering spirit if it *wants* to return, and if you are still in any doubt, instruct your totem beast or power animal to travel further into the inner worlds and make this enquiry on your behalf.

DEATH AND THE SHAMAN

You will find many references in shamanic literature to the near-death experience, which lies at the heart of a great deal of trainee-shamanic practice. The idea behind this is that through such experiences the apprentice shaman is enabled to move closer to the Otherworld, and even to cross the border for a brief time.

This is clearly important. Nevertheless, it is no longer necessary to face death in quite so literal a way. Through vision and in dream the shaman visits the Otherworld and returns richly laden with the treasures of wisdom and knowledge. We should be working towards the death of the self-limiting self, and to its replacement with a fully empowered version which is able to relate to *both* the worlds, and to move between one and the other with confidence and ease. It is in this light that the following instruction should be understood. It is not a literal, physical death which is being experienced here, but a spiritual awakening to the possibilities inherent within the soul of the shaman. (A more detailed consideration of this will be found in *The Celtic Book of the Dead* by Caitlín Matthews.)

The Soul's Rebirth

Prepare yourself for a journey. Close your eyes and see before you one of the entrances to the Otherworld: a fairy thorn bush, a cave mouth, or an ancient tree with a hole beneath its roots leading down . . . Follow the way until you reach the inner realm. A path leads before you to the entrance to a hall of timbers and golden thatch. Within awaits the queen of that place, who offers you a cup. This is the Dark Drink of Forgetting, offered to those who enter the Otherworld for the last time, so that they will forget the life they have left behind. So, too, as you drink, you forget for a time who or what you are, and wander through the Many-coloured Land until you meet a tall, dark-faced man who leads you to a hut beside marshes. Strange lights hover above the dank waters and marsh-birds call long and sadly. The man leads you into the hut, which you see is really a smithy, with anvil, bellows and tongs laid ready. Over a great fire stands a huge blackened cauldron, filled with boiling liquid. Silently the man builds up the fire even higher and applies the bellows. Then suddenly, swift as light, the smith catches you and cuts off your head with a great sword. Then he chops your body into pieces, which he flings into the mouth of the cauldron . . . You feel yourself beginning to dissolve, but as the flesh falls from your bones you feel your essence carried upwards on the steam which rises from the mouth of the cauldron. Then you find that you have wings and have in fact become a bird. You stretch your pinions and take delight in the wonder of flight . . . But soon the earth begins to draw you back, and you drift slowly down on the air until you are standing on the ground . . . but on four feet, not two, for now you are an otter. You race through deep underbush towards the scent of water and fling yourself into a fast-flowing river . . . Carried down-stream your keen senses detect a fish swimming before you in the murky depths. You give chase . . . but suddenly you are no longer a creature of fur and feet, but a fish yourself, sliding through the water on silvery fins. Ahead light shines down through the water and you are drawn towards it . . . You burst out in a great leap . . . and find that you are yourself again, and whole, and that you have leapt from the cauldron . . . Swiftly the smith catches you and flings you onto the anvil, where he beats you with his hammers until you are tempered like the finest steel. Then he takes out your eyes and resets them at once, but in a different way so that you can see more clearly than before. And he takes out your tongue and hammers it on the anvil and replaces it so that you can speak with animals and birds and fish. And lastly he pierces your ears with his tongs so that forever after you can hear the voices of all creatures and understand them . . . Then, holding you firmly in his great arms, he dips you swiftly into the cauldron and sets you upon your feet. All this seems to have taken but a moment. As though waking from a dream you find yourself standing again in the hall of the queen of the Otherworld. Only now she offers you a new cup from which to drink, containing the White Drink of Fosterage, which confirms you in your restored and reborn self . . . Slowly the scene begins to fade and you return to mundane reality, in peace and harmony and with many new insights.

You should rest, drink and eat after this meditation, which will have a deep and lasting effect upon you for some time; you have been truly 're-made' by the smith, the most ancient and primal of the Lords of the Otherworld. Like the experiences of all shamans at this stage of training, it marks a point of great change and new beginnings.

8 The Keys of Divination

'Maeve scanned the woman and said,
'At this time, and here, what doest thou?'
The young woman answered: 'I reveal
thy chance and thy fortunes.'

Tain bo Cuailgne

THE BURNING SHAMAN

TO BE A SHAMAN is to be inspired, inspirited, to feel the power of the spirit-world within you. To divine means to listen for and to hear the voice of god. These two facts together form the basis of an understanding of what it means to foretell the future, and to see beyond the narrow view of existence from which most of us take stock of our lives. One of the prime functions of the shaman in any age or place is to divine the future, either for the tribe as a whole, or for individuals. It is most likely that the modern shaman or shamanka will be required to exercise this particular skill for single people.

The search for omens and their meaningful interpretations is one that has long been recognized as a major concern of human beings. Ellen Ettlinger, in an article on the subject of 'Omens and Celtic Warfare', sums this up precisely:

The life of primitive man depended upon his unceasingly vigilant attitude towards the phenomena of nature. Among these were uncanny incidents, strange coincidences or vivid dream-impressions which took hold of his imagination. By pure intuition and without any analogy man interpreted a stirring natural happening as a warning of trouble ahead. Similar or recurrent experiences caused the attribution of . . . foreboding to a particular event.

The newly won knowledge was passed on to the medicine-man who handed the facts and the meaning of the 'omen' down to his successor. As time went on the functions of the medicine-man gradually separated more and more from each other and developed along their own lines. Magicians, diviners, leeches, judges, and poets emerged and were initiated into the omen-language in order to satisfy the requirements of their respective activities.

The Celts had many different methods of divination, some of which are dealt with below. However, the most significant and best known are:

Tenm Laida: Illumination of Song
Dichetal Do Chennaib: Extempore Incantation
Imbas Forosna: Wisdom that Illuminates

The translations given here are, for the most part, accepted, though on closer examination they are less than satisfactory. *Tenm Laida* and *Dichetal do Chennaib* are frequently confused with each other. *Tenm* is sometimes said to mean 'chewing the thumb' or even 'the burning thumb', but a more accurate and clearer translation is 'burning song'. If we look for a moment at each one of these arcane disciplines in turn, we shall see that they are less impenetrable than they at first seem, and that they can also have relevance for practising shamans today.

Tenm Laida

This is in fact the burning song of the chant, the power of which can change the consciousness of both the practitioner and those who are within hearing. Chanting energizes the body and stills the mind. You can take almost any of the chants from the vast repository of lore collected by Alexander Carmichael in the *Carmina Gadelica* and repeat them with variations. You can also make up your own chant, or a rhythmic murmur if you find that words do not come easily. The use of chanting quickly puts you into a state of mind in which you can break out of ordinary reality and find your way into the inner realms.

The chant should consist of a brief and memorable phrase, generally not more than two or three lines long (it is difficult to remember more) which can be repeated for as long as necessary. Several examples are given throughout this book, but you should begin to make up your own as soon as possible. Once you have tried chanting for an hour or more you will find that you can do it for much longer, and that your mind will be utterly free and at peace.

Dichetal do Chennaib

This is said to mean either 'cracking open the nuts of wisdom' or 'incantation on the bones of the fingers'. The first suggests a reference to the familiar story of the well-head, by the side of which grow nine hazels whose nuts contain all the wisdom of the Otherworld. The second could even be a reference to the 'alphabet of the poets', the mysterious inscriptions known as ogham. A third explanation is found in the early Irish law tract known as *Senchus Mor*, where it is written, under the heading of *Dichetal*, that when a poet (for which read prophet or shaman) wanted to know about something he 'placed his staff upon the person's body or upon his head, and found out the name of his father, and mother, and discovered every unknown thing that was proposed to him . . .'

This suggests a technique involving the acquisition of ancestral wisdom through physical contact. There are numerous references in the later traditions of seership to those who could divine simply by touching the person who desired an answer. Some degree of psychism is probably required for this technique; the following are two suggestions of ways in which this method of divination could be practised today.

You will need a staff, or poet's wand, which need be no more than a reasonably straight piece of wood, but can also be a fairly elaborate carved stick or wand. The idea is that you will charge this with your energy and then use it to divine the answer to a question. Sit in your sacred circle with the stick across your knees, and chant a power song over it. This could be something like:

> Wood be strong,
> Wood have power
> Wood be strong
> From this hour.

When you feel that the wand is sufficiently charged you may use it as follows.

Get the person posing the question to put his or her left hand on the staff, about two-thirds of the way down. Then put your right hand above it, and get him or her to put the right hand above yours. Now put your left hand above that, so that you are holding the staff between you as in Figure 29.

Now close your eyes and let your mind go blank; after a while an image or images should appear, which will be the answer to the particular question. With practice, and as your shamanic skills develop, you should be able to get good results.

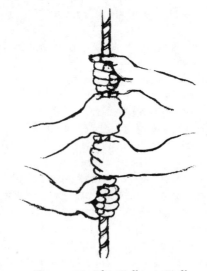

Figure 29. The Talking Staff

A related, and very ancient, method, is known simply as:

Watching the Road

The object of this is to enable the shaman to foresee certain future events, such as birth, as well as the causes of illness or death. From within your sacred place you enter into a trance in which you perceive the road of the gods, a network of branching, different-coloured roads which criss-cross the heavens. These starry pathways are the routes by which the spirits who communicate with the gods pass to and fro, and if the shaman has sufficient courage he or she may travel upon these and may even stop and question those he or she encounters. In this way knowledge of many things is gained, and the shaman is able to see links in the chain of creation as well as events that are to come, more clearly. If and when you feel that you are ready to tread this road, it is advisable to take your totem beast with you and to observe the following rules.

Firstly, whoever or whatever you meet may be disinclined to speak with you for a number of reasons. Never force yourself upon such beings; always ask permission politely before you put your question, and never repeat the same question . . .

Imbas Forosna

Of the three methods this is the only one which seems to translate accurately: literally 'illumination', and as such it is the most interesting since it is concerned with a technique of divination (or more properly of inspiration) which we know a good deal about, and which can still be practised successfully today. This is part of the extraordinary Celtic understanding of the contrast between darkness and light, and the effect which prolonged subjection to one, followed by exposure to the other, could produce in those with the necessary training.

It is also apparent that both water and light were seen as direct conductors, not only of healing, but also of information from beneath the ground. Numerous examples appear in Celtic literature of omens or precognitive dreams vouchsafed beside rivers or springs. One ancient text says that poets thought 'that the place where poetry was revealed was upon the brink of water' (*Immacallam in da Thuarad*). In the poetry of Taliesin there are more references to water than to any other element, and this reflects the complex matter of visionary insight as it connects with both darkness and light, as in the story of Nechtan's Well.

Throughout Celtic literature, from the fifth to the eighteenth centuries, there are references to seers who allowed themselves to be concealed in dark places for varying periods of time. They were then suddenly brought forth into bright daylight or firelight, and promptly delivered extensive prophetic insights.

There have been various attempts to explain this phenomenon as everything from sensory deprivation to outright sorcery. The truth of the matter is far simpler. To be completely deprived of light for any length of time throws the subject back upon the most profound areas of the psyche. Going into the dark is reminiscent of re-entering the womb of creation/inspiration, and of preparing for a deeper descent – into death and rebirth. Small wonder then that the seers of the Celtic world could return from a visionary journey after such an experience with a deep and lasting garnering of wisdom. In our own time we can recreate this journey in visualization and dream, entering the inner worlds in order to discover not only ourselves, but news of others. The harsh laws of initiation, rest and trial return to us as we make the descent into the dark places of the soul, the same soul from which the images of our inner sacred life arise.

Thus most shamans who are also diviners work in the dark. This enables them to see more clearly, and cuts out the distractions of the everyday world. The following exercise utilizes this practice of deriving illumination from darkness; it combines the techniques of visualization and sensory deprivation.

The Blindfold Hunter

First you must have something to ask, a question which requires answering with some degree of urgency. Set up your circle in a place which can be completely darkened. Take a light with you so that you can see to write down the answer if or when one comes. Now settle yourself in the shaman's posture and bind your eyes with a scarf; you must be in utter darkness. Once you are settled begin to chant, very softly and steadily:

> Dark is dark,
> Light is light
> Dark is dark,
> Light is light.

Keep this up until you begin to lose touch with reality. You can see nothing but the darkness, which enfolds you utterly. You could be anywhere in the universe, you could be the only person left . . .

Now begin to concentrate on the question. Look at it from every conceivable angle. Try framing it in your head in as many ways as possible. Make a new chant of it and chant it aloud . . .

After a time you begin to feel that you are sinking through the floor. But is there a floor there at all? And, if there is, and you are sinking down, where are you going to?

It is usual, at this point, to feel some dissociation and confusion. You will probably start to wonder how long you have been there (wherever 'there' is . . .). You may start to sweat, or feel very cold, or that your bowels are turning to liquid . . . If you can ride this part out you will begin to feel very light and transparent, though of course there is no light to shine through you . . .

Then in the distance, you seem to see something. At first you think it is an illusion, because there is no light to reveal anything . . . But the feeling grows stronger, and with it comes a new certainty. There, in the distance, is light! Only a dim greyness which would not, in normal circumstances, pass for light at all, but it is enough to show you that you are sitting on a grassy knoll in the middle of an unknown landscape . . .

You strain your senses to 'see' where the light is coming from. There, below the mound, you gradually make out the shape of a well-head. The light is coming from within the well . . . So desperate are you by now that you scramble down to the lip of the well and look in . . .

At once there comes such a blast of light that you reel back from the well, blinded by the violence of the illumination. It is at that moment, confused and befuddled, caught between the two extremes of uttermost darkness and brilliant light, that you hear the answer to your question, as loudly as though it had been shouted up to you from within the well . . . Desperately you scrabble at the blindfold which you are suddenly aware is around your eyes . . .

It may take a few minutes to actually complete this part of the exercise. When you remove the scarf you will not be able to see very much. Make sure you have paper and pen, or a tape recorder, close to hand, and retain the answer in your head until you are able to write it down or record it. Take a rest and have a drink when you are ready. This exercise, simple though it may seem, is both tiring and occasionally disturbing. Make sure you eat and earth yourself as soon as possible.

In this way, we enter the womb of the earth, listen for a time to her wisdom, then re-emerge, reborn, into the world of manifestation. There we are met with light, the outpouring of metaphysical understanding which, if we are not blinded by it, we can receive, transforming it through a synthesis of soul and body. At this juncture, received notions of 'light' and 'dark' vanish, and the interaction is so profound that we cannot even see it. What we experience, instead is a universal sense of 'right' feeling, of complete awareness. The world around us is transformed. We have returned from the Otherworld with good news for ourselves and our fellow creatures. The ultimate prophetic reality is made possible.

CLOUD WATCHING

The Celts believed that clouds, driven and shaped by the winds, could tell them things they needed to know. They gave each of the winds a name and a colour, and in the clouds they saw mysteries reflected. There was even a special term for the practice of cloud-watching – *neladoracht*: divination by clouds. The following exercise is a way of changing your perceptions of the outer world, and entering a state of being which is both meditative and active.

Cloud Dreams

Find a hollow stone or shallow dish and fill it with fresh water from a stream. Look into the water and see reflected there the clouds above you. Decide on your question and watch the clouds for a time, still concentrating on the question. Then turn and lie on your back and look up at the clouds properly. Observe their formation, the faces and shapes that appear in them, and apply this to the question you asked. With a little practice you may be surprised at the depths of the answers you receive.

THE OGHAM SECRET

The most problematic of the divinatory techniques discussed here is that of ogham, also known as 'the secret language of poets'. We know a good deal about ogham, and the ways in which it worked; the difficulties lie in the vast range of symbolic reference required to be able to make use of the system in the way our Celtic forebears would have done.

Essentially, ogham is an alphabet, consisting of twenty letters with five additional characters: these last five were probably added on to the original series at a later date. Ogham had several uses, notably as a language of memorial upon pillar-stone inscriptions. Some three hundred ogham-inscribed stones have been discovered in Britain and

Symbol	Ogham name	Letter	Tree
	Beithe	b	birch
	Luis	l	elm/rowan
	Fearn	f	alder
	Saile	s	willow
	Nuin	n	ash
	(H)Uathe	h	whitethorn/hawthorn
	Duir	d	oak
	Tinne	t	holly/elderberry
	Coll	c	hazel
	Quert	q	aspen/apple
	Muinn	m	vine/mulberry
	Gort	g	fir/ivy
	Negetal	ng	broom/fern
	Straif	str	blackthorn
	Ruis	r	elder
	Ailm	a	fir/pine
	Ohn	o	furze/ash/gorse
	Ur	u	thorn/heather
	Edhadh	e	yew/aspen
	Ido	i	service tree/yew
	Ebadh	eba	elecampane/aspen
	Oir	oi	spindle tree
	Uilleand	ui	ivy/honeysuckle
	Iphin	io	pine/gooseberry
	Emancoll/phagos	ae	witchhazel/beech

Figure 30. The Ogham Alphabet

Ireland, dating between the fourth and the seventh centuries AD: the inscriptions are incised on the stones' edges and generally read from the bottom to the top. Most of them record the name of a notable person, but little more.

The medieval Irish text, the *Book of Ballymote* has a treatise upon ogham which reveals it to have been used as a primer for poets and scholars, giving many complex kennings and epithets which have magical nuances. These kennings or shamanic word-meanings are immediately perceptible in the names of the letters, each of which is the Gaelic name of a tree, for example D = duir (oak), R = ruis (elder). These names are still used in the modern Gaelic language. Ogham is also frequently called 'the tree alphabet'.

In ancient times, ogham was probably used as a mnemonic reference to complex correspondences which might have been used as a divinatory system. Robert Macalister suggests that the arrangement of the ogham into fivefold groupings might have indicated its use as a manual code which could be used by initiates: much of Robert Graves' *The White Goddess* is an exposition of this theory. However, ogham was used in divination, according to the *Book of Ballymote*, as a means of divining the sex of an unborn child. There are also references elsewhere to throwing billets of wood, previously inscribed with oghamic letters, to judge the guilt or innocence of a person accused of crimes to which there are no witnesses. The outline of an alternative ogham divinatory system is given in this chapter: it is one which you can flesh out by shamanic journeying to recover the fuller meanings of each letter.

The complete ogham alphabet is shown on page 160.

It will be seen that there are a number of variants concerning attribution of a certain tree or bush to a particular letter. The order has also changed throughout its long development, so that we cannot always be sure of its original form. But ogham itself is thought to have been invented by the god of inspiration and poetry, Ogma Sun-Face. It is a sun-wisdom and its light, like that of Nechtan's Well, can blind us to its true meaning if we are not careful. A further clue may exist in a series of riddling 'glosses' to the letters, found in a medieval manuscript.

Alphabet of Word-oghams of Mac ind Oic

Glaisium cnis	Most silvery of skin
Cara ceathra	Friend of cattle
Comet lachta	Guarding of milk
Luth bech	Activity of bees
Bag ban	Flight of women

Banadh gnuisi	Blanching of face
Gres sair	Carpenter's work
Smir guaili	Fires of coal
Cara bloisc	Friend of cracking
Brigh annum	Force of the man
Aruusc n-arrligh	Condition of slaughter
Mednercc	Ivy
Etiud midach	Robe of Physicians
Moridrun	Increasing of secrets
Ruamna dreach	Redness of faces
Tosach fregra	Beginning of an answer
Feithim saire	Smoothest of work
Siladh clann	Growing of plants
Comainm carat	Synonym for a friend
Crinem feada	Most withered of wood
Cosc lobair	Corrective of a sick man
Li crotha	Beauty of form
Cubat n-oll	Great equal-length
Amram blais	Most wonderful of taste

We shall see a possible use for this in a moment. For the present note that the letters are once again attributed to a god, this time the god of eternal youth. Consider also that the shaman-poets must have had to learn such lists by heart, enabling them to speak a language intelligible only to those similarly trained in the bardic/shamanic mysteries.

Other lists exist which equate the letters with parts of the body (finger, nose, thigh, hand, foot, for example) and were used in a similar fashion; touching the part of the body in question would indicate to those who understood a word or letter which could then be interpreted. Other kinds of ogham include sow, shield, river-pool, fortress, bird, colour, king, water, dog and food.

The shaman-poet therefore had to be familiar with a vast range of knowledge; not only the general meaning of the ogham characters, but also the many secret meanings which lay behind them. The interpretation of the letters thus rested on a full spectrum of knowledge in which the relationship of the letters (or letter) to each other, to the remainder of the inscription, and to the context in which they were found, all had to be taken into account.

Ogham divination thus really requires a book to itself, and will be dealt with in greater detail in a later volume. For the present I offer you a few clues. (It is an old and well-tried method of shamanic teaching to set puzzles which the apprentices had to solve on their own).

In *The Wooing of Etain* the letters are described as *eochra ecsi* (keys of knowledge), and this probably equates with a passage from the *Seanchus Mor* concerning a method of judgement known as *crannchur* or 'casting the woods'. According to this, if there was doubt as to the identity of a murderer, thief or adulterer, three wooden lots were placed in a bag and drawn forth one by one. According to the order in which they were laid down a judgement was made.

This suggests that a system once existed in which a number of billets of wood, perhaps each inscribed with a letter of the ogham alphabet, were placed in a bag, shaken up and drawn out at random. According to the way they fell a reading would then be made. The problem that faces us today is what meanings to ascribe to the letters, beyond that of their tree-names. Fortunately, two clues are to be found among the manuscripts dealing with ogham.

We have already seen one of the lists of poetic 'glosses' to the letters, and at first glance this may seem to add little to our understanding. However, other lists exist, and one of these contains some surprises.

Word Oghams of Morann Mac Main

Feocus foltchain	Faded trunk and fair hair	(Age)
Li sula	Delight of eye	(Love)
Airinach Fian	Shield of warriors	(Defence)
Li n-aimbi	Dead colour	(Death)
Corsdad sida	Checking of peace	(Opposition)
Conal cuan	Pack of wolves	(Challenge)
Ardam dossaibh	Highest of bushes	(Seeking)
Trian	Third of . . .	
Cainiu fedaib	Fairest of trees	(Beauty)
Clithar mb aiscaill	Shelter of a hind	(Caring)
Tresim fedma	Strongest of efforts	(Effort)
Millsiu feraib	Sweeter than grasses	(Satisfaction)
Luth legha	A physician's strength	(Healing)
Tresim ruamna	Strongest red	(Anger)
Tinnem ruccae	Intense burning	(Inspiration)
Ardam iactadh	Loudest groaning	(Misery)
Congnamaigh echraide	Helper of horses	(Travel)
Uaraib adbaib	In cold dwellings	(Fear)
Ergnaid fid	Distinguished wood	(Insight)
Siniu fedhaib	Oldest of woods	(Wisdom)
Snamchain fheda	Most buoyant of wood	(Ability)
Sruitem aicdi	Most venerable structure	(Truth)

Tutmur fid uilleann	Woodbine the strong	(Discovery)
Millsim feda	Sweetest of wood	(Taste)
Luad saethaig	Sign of a weary one	(Exhaustion)

A little intuition yields the above 'translations' which form an interesting index of abilities, emotions and qualities, all of which were experienced at one time or another by the shaman (see Chapter 5 and elsewhere). Could it be that here we have a list of 'meanings' for the ogham letters? If so, the possibilities of divination by ogham immediately becomes apparent.

A second important clue lies in the arrangement of the letters around the wheel. In a medieval manuscript known as *The Book of Ballymote*, there are several pages of ogham scripts and inscriptions. Among these is a diagram labelled 'Fionn's Window'. We may safely assume that this refers to Fionn Mac Cumhail, who shared the illumination of wisdom also discovered by Taliesin.

The 'window' is interesting. Five is a sacred number, and the window arranges the five sets of five ogham letters around the wheel in a specific pattern of five circles. Thus *beithe, luis, fearn, saile* and *nuin* are in the north: *uathe, duir, tinne, coll* and *quert* are in the east: *muinn, gort, negetal, straif* and *ruis* are in the south, and *ailm, ohn, ur, edhadh* and *ido* are in the west. The five remaining letters, *ebadh, oir, uilleand, iphin* and *phagos* are placed at north-east, south-east, south-west and north-west respectively.

From this we learn the positions of the letters around the Sacred Wheel. Possibly Iphin, the extra letter in the south-west would go at the centre, according to its appropriateness to the diviner. When the paths from the eight-spoked wheel outlined in Chapter 5 are placed side by side with the cryptic lists of word ogham described above, an interesting pattern emerges. If we then break up this list into fives and ascribe them to the directions given in Fionn's window, we arrive at the following:

North
(Path of Finding Wisdom)

Faded trunk and fair hair	(Age)
Delight of eye	(Love)
Shield of Warriors	(Defence)
Dead colour	(Death)
Checking of peace	(Opposition)

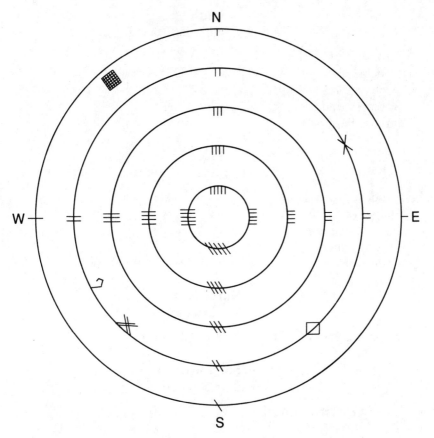

Figure 31. Fionn's Window

East
(Path of Opening the Way)

Pack of wolves	(Challenge)
Highest of bushes	(Seeking)
Trian	(Third of . . .)
Fairest of trees	(Beauty)
Shelter of a hind	(Protection)

South
(Path of Coming into Being)

Strongest of efforts	(Effort)
Sweeter than grasses	(Satisfaction)
A physician's strength	(Healing)
Strongest red	(Anger)
Intense burning	(Inspiration)

West
(Path of Passing Within)

Loudest groaning	(Misery)
Helper of horses	(Travel)
In cold dwellings	(Fear)
Distinguished wood	(Insight)
Oldest of woods	(Wisdom)

North-east
(Path of Inspiration)

Most buoyant of wood	(Ability)

South-east
(Path of Strength)

Most venerable structure	(Truth)

South-west
(Path of Insight)

Woodbine the strong	(Discovery)
Sweetest of wood	(Taste)

North-west
(Path of Cleansing)

Sign of a weary one	(Exhaustion)

You will see that the overlay of material here is remarkable. With these keys at your disposal you should now be able to move on to divining with ogham, and next you should do one of two things:

1. Go out into the wilds and collect a slip of wood from each of the twenty-five trees represented by the ogham alphabet, or

2. Buy some lengths of dowelling and cut these into billets approximately 3 or 4 inches long.

Whichever you decide to do (clearly the first option is the better one, but it is not always possible to collect such a variety of woods) you should then carve each piece with the appropriate ogham letter. Keep these in a special bag and when you want to make an augury proceed as follows.

Take out three or more of the wooden slips and 'cast' them at random on the ground. An alternative method is to design a more elaborate chart on paper or cloth, based on Fionn's window, on which you can cast the woods. You should then make a reading from their positions, and perhaps make a journey to the path which corresponds to that on the eight-spoked wheel. (For some alternatives see the resources list at the end of this book.)

There are many possibilities to explore here, and I hope to investigate the subject further in the future. When you have worked for a time with the system outlined here, refer to the list on p. 161 and use your own shamanic skill and insight to interpret *this* list. See where and how it fits around the wheel and, devise a means of interpretation for yourself.

From this you will see that, elusive as the Celtic methods of divination may appear, they do yield to an inspirational approach. Essentially, all forms of divinatory work arise from a deep communion with the Otherworld. This should have been achieved through your earlier shamanic-training, in which case even the most obscure method of divining will prove to be no obstacle. You need only consider the applications of this knowledge, which should, along with all Otherworldly gifts, be treated with respect and used only for honourable purposes.

9 Mythlines

The red, the heat, the flame, the fire, the
sacred fire without end. Your
grandfather lit it for your father who is
lighting it for you now . . . tend this
fire: pass it on to the next generation,
to the son you will have sometime, so
that he can pass it on to his children.

Leonard Crow Dog, Lakota Elder

THE FIRST STORY-TELLERS

SHAMANS WERE THE FIRST STORY-TELLERS, who spun the myths which still
affect us today. The best way to teach is still by the parable, which is a
special kind of story. You, as a shaman, should learn as many stories,
folk-tales, apocryphal yarns and myths as possible. But the most important story you have to learn is your own. Not only do you have to learn
it, but also how to tell it as well, to the most difficult audience of all –
your self.

Everything holds the quality of myth. Life is full of mythic allusions,
which you, the shaman story-teller, must learn to sing. For this reason
you should continue your personal exploration of the infinite inner
dimensions of the cosmos. Much of this has been done already, but it is
just a beginning; if you intend to follow the shaman's path, many years
of inner journeying lie before you. And, whenever you enter the
Otherworld and return, you will have another story to tell. The following are only a few thoughts as to the ways in which you can integrate
these mysteries with your own life.

Conventional religious practice, however valuable, often fails because
it does not answer humanity's deep need for myth. As Alberto Villoldo

says in the book *The Four Winds*, all priesthoods are no more than 'caretakers of myth', while the shamans go out into the deep regions of the Otherworld and return with new myths in the making. These they preserve, as they have done since time immemorial. You, in telling your story, are producing new myths to guide our lives.

THE NEED OF THE WORLD

The great mythographer Joseph Campbell said, on more than one occasion, that he believed a new mythology for our time was not only needed but on its way, though he could not say what form it would take. I believe that it may well be a shamanic mythos, and that in seeking out the myths and teachings of our own Celtic tradition we shall begin to build our own part of that mythos. Shamanism fits the need of the world so well precisely *because* it is founded upon a common set of perceptions, and because it relates so well to the world about us.

This being the case what can we, as Celtic shamans, do to add our own voices to the evolving story? We must learn some of the wonderful stories to be found in ancient Celtic literature. These are not always so inaccessible as you might think, and they represent the best method of getting in touch with the native tradition of these islands. Examples will be found listed in the bibliography and more extensively in various other books by John and Caitlín Matthews. The great collection known as *The Mabinogion* is readily available, as are volumes of Irish myths, and Scottish and Breton stories and folk-tales. You could also try to find some of the rarer and less accessible texts and, once you come across one that seems to possess a shamanic content (or which is relevant to you), try learning it by heart.

This is not as difficult as it sounds. It is not a matter of using the same words every time, but of knowing the components of the story and the way they fit together. Once you have grasped this you can tell the stories aloud to anyone who will listen — and surely everyone loves a good story!

ANOTHER STORY

In time you will be ready to begin telling another story — your own. Your entire life is a story, and there is much to be learned from reviewing it from time to time. Try relating small episodes aloud to yourself, just as if you were repeating an anecdote to a circle of friends at the dinner table. Only this time hold nothing back, as you might be tempted to do in other circumstances, and consciously look for the hidden patterns that inform all our lives. Watch out for the significant references to things you may not be aware of yourself. You will be surprised at the revelatory nature of things you 'remember' when you do so.

Now develop this idea a little. Take an episode from your life, the outcome of which was less than satisfactory. Re-tell it in one of the following ways:

1. A hero tale.
2. A chance encounter with fate.
3. A significant part of a larger pattern.

If you want to get a friend or partner to do this, so much the better. The results can be profound, moving, and sometimes hilariously funny (laughter is one of the shaman's most powerful tools).

Here is a fictional example of the kind of thing I mean.

> I went for a job interview the other day, but when I got there I was so nervous that I could hardly speak. I failed to get the job even though I am not normally tongue-tied.

The same story, told as a hero tale, goes as follows:

> I went for a job interview the other day. I kept silent for much of the time and had only to look at the boss to get his attention. I used my skills as a listener — being able to hear an ant scratching itself a hundred miles away — and he was so impressed that he gave me the job.

From this you can learn an important shamanic lesson in self-esteem and empowerment. Another way to do this is to take a genuinely empowering anecdote which actually happened to you, and to retell it to yourself, consciously looking for hidden meanings. We do this for ourselves already, in dream or visionary journey or meditation. Relating the story of such a key event as part of an ongoing journey is extremely valuable. Even if you do not fully understand the episode, you may find that it becomes clearer either as you tell it, or a few days or even weeks later. The important thing is to tell the story to yourself again and again, until it is truly part of your consciousness.

Still another way to work with the story is to record it in the form of symbols. This is the idea behind the painting of drum or shield or stone as described earlier. By reducing a significant personal experience to a shamanic whole you are teaching yourself a great deal that might otherwise never become apparent.

Finally, another way of using the story is to take one of your favourite tales from the Celtic tradition, and to retell that story with yourself as the main protagonist. How would *you* deal with the problems and challenges which face the hero/heroine? To put yourself into such a story is, at the same time, to feel a sense of belonging to the tradition, and to learn from your own interaction with the events it relates.

I have left one of the most important teachings almost until last: how to tell your own story. The Celts loved stories and had a professional body of people, bards and seanachies, whose task it was to learn hundreds of them by heart. Many of these are now lost to us, though we know the names of some, and these are listed here. Why not write your own story to fit one or more of these titles? You may think you have no aptitude for story-telling, but most people can manage it, even if its only what happened to them today, or a joke. But more important than this is learning to tell your own story every day of your life. What is your story? What kind of person does it make you? Are you a warrior or a healer or a singer or a traveller? These are only a few of the possible roles you might fill — maybe several in your lifetime. You have to ask yourself what kind of a story you are living in, and then you can start telling it, maybe only to yourself at first. You might write it down and read it over every few weeks. Then see if you can spot the patterns which lie just beneath the surface.

Lost Celtic Tales

The Fosterage of the House of the Two Vessels
The Enchanted Hall of the Rowan Tree
Hound, Son of the Smith
The Adventure with the Naked Savage
The Bird of Sweet Music
How Cormac Got His Branch
The Wandering of the Empress
The Quest of the Rock of Scarlet

These are ancient stories which were once told in the halls of Celtic kings. Working with them will draw you closer to the spirits of the Celtic people, and of their shaman poets and story-tellers. These may not mean very much to you initially, but if you meditate on the titles individually you may well be surprised at what stirs within you.

Story-telling as a form of teaching has been used since the beginning of time. The parables of Christ and of the Celtic monks were stories to teach us how to live. Among the native people of North America, the Aborigines of Australia and the Sami singers of Lappland, for example, there is a virtually endless fund of stories which tell about recreation and continuance of the sacred, and the relationship of people to it. The old traditional Celtic stories and songs recited by the bards were meant for both pleasure and instruction. The poems of Taliesin contain a world of secrets waiting to be explored. The nature poems and the magical poems of the bards can tell us more than a hundred books. The stories and folk-tales of the Celts tell us about the Otherworld, about this world, about ourselves. It is a good idea to learn at least one story by heart; it doesn't matter if the words are always the same, just so long as the elements of the story are firmly entrenched within you. Then you can tell it to anyone who would like to hear it, and you may be surprised how many people will be interested. Try it out on your children; I have been telling magical stories to my son since he was old enough to understand my words. Sometimes he understands them better than I do!

Listen to the old stories then, and you will be surprised how much you learn. Many of the old teachings are contained within them, just waiting to be pulled out and practised. After a time you may find that new stories suggest themselves to you, maybe containing elements from the old tales which reveal themselves in new ways. Write down the story, and then try to learn it. If you can retain it *without* writing it down so much the better, because then it will really be a part of you.

THE POWER OF THE ANCESTORS

The deepest and most ancient source of visionary knowledge, and of the great story, are the ancestors. They are both the founders and inner guides of an individual race, who embody the cultural patternings upon which many traditions are founded. They are sometimes literally members of a particular family, but more often are ancient dreamers whose sleep holds images of the future, which are contained as potential in the past. It is possible to tune into the energy of these beings, and to learn from them, but it should also be understood that they do not always resonate well with present human concerns or conditions.

There are examples of ancestral teachings throughout Celtic mythology, and they form a large part of the teachings contained here. The Roman historian Tertullian recorded that the Celts used to sleep on the graves of their ancestors to obtain wisdom. It is not suggested that this is necessarily a good thing to do today. Rather, we may see that certain ancient sites contain memories of previous times, and that many of them still have guardians attached to them. The best account of the ancestral traditions is to be found in the writings of R. J. Stewart, to which the interested reader is recommended; the following are a few further notes and suggestions on ways of seeking ancestral wisdom.

Respect for the ancestors is still practised at Samhain in the Celtic world, when the doors between the worlds are open. But it is appropriate that they should be remembered more frequently; it is good to honour and acknowledge them, as well as to ask for their guidance. Not all ancestors are willing to help us; some are caught in webs of their own making, and seek to enmesh us also. You should travel with the blessings and the protection and guidance of your totem and/or inner shaman. You may already know or communicate with a loved ancestor who has proved trustworthy. But remember that many ancestral patterns, good and bad, are inherited and pass on in our own families. Contemplate your family and see what restrictive, unrealistic or atavistic patterns exist there. Healing and stemming these forces requires great integrity and clear motivation. However, the ancestors generally act as guardians or repositories for ancient wisdom: they can be consulted about matters to do with the land and with families, and can act as protectors and watch-dogs for your home.

Honouring the ancestors is also very important, and can be done in a number of ways. Simply thinking of your own family can be important. You can also make a small ancestral shrine, including a photo of your own ancestors, or use a picture of a site which has strong ancestral associations. The shrine can contain other objects which strike you as particularly symbolic: a cord set in a spiral pattern, a flat stone on which you can write messages to the ancestors, a basket of stones taken from many different places. An offering dish of honey, sweet-cake or beer can be placed there also (but make sure you replenish it regularly!)

At your ancestral shrine, make offerings, have conversations, tell jokes (the ancestors like news, gossip and humour) and ask advice. The important thing is to establish a feeling of friendship and rapport across the divide of time and place. If you then wish to go more deeply into the matter of ancestral wisdom there are other possibilities.

THE OLD ONES' WISDOM

Many of the ancient stories are themselves ways into the deep ancestral past of the Celts. One in particular holds a great richness of material: 'The Settling of the Manor of Tara', edited by R. I. Best. This extraordinary text bears such an incredible amount of mythological meaning, both about the power of story and the way that ancestral wisdom is passed on, that it is worth summarizing here.

Ancient Ireland was divided into five parts, of which Tara was the largest and most central. The chieftains of the other four areas gathered together to discuss the rights of this. The division of the land had taken place in a very distant time, and to find out why they applied to various elders, poets of greater age and dignity. Finally they called upon Fintan, who was believed to be the most ancient and wisest man in all the land. However, old as he was, Fintan told of those older still, namely Tuan mac Cairell, who, like Taliesin, underwent transformations into beast and bird, in whose shape he lived for a hundred years before changing once again. The other character mentioned by Fintan is Trefuilngid Treochair (Strong Upholder of the Three Keys) whose task was to cause the sun to rise and set each day, and who had been present at an earlier meeting of elders when the original divisions of the land had been decided. This Trefuilngid had recalled for these earlier people the very birth of their history. In other words, through a series of references to ever earlier and wiser ancestors, the people of the present time (in the story) learn of their own past, recalled far beyond the memory of any one man.

This was one of the principal tasks of the shamans: to remember the past of their land and people, and to recall the wisdom of those who went before. The Celts themselves did not keep any written records until fairly late in their history, so that all the myths and legends, folklore and wisdom we have today were transmitted orally for many hundreds of years.

The lesson we can learn from this concerns the preservation of our own traditional wisdom and the recovery of that which has been forgotten. There are ways to discover this which you will find for yourself if you continue to work with the ancestors. One method combines the idea of the oldest ancestors mentioned in 'The Settling of the Manor of Tara' with the totemic helpers described in Chapter 3. The theme is an ancient one, called 'The Oldest Animals', where someone in need of help or knowledge applies to a succession of ever more ancient beings. This visualization follows the sequence of an old Irish poem which deals with this theme.

The Oldest Animals

Close your eyes and prepare to journey to an older time, when the wisdom of the lands was remembered by the wise.

You find yourself standing in front of a little round hut with a thatched roof and a skin curtain for a door. All around is a landscape of rolling hills, interspersed with rivers and woodland. As though you were expected the curtain is pulled aside and before you stands a man who seems as old as the world itself. Shrunken and wizened he may be, but his eyes are still keen and sharp and filled with intelligence. 'Who comes to disturb my rest?' he demands, but not angrily, more in resignation. You give your name and ask his. 'That', he replies, 'may take time to tell, for I am the product of many people, and though my given name is Fintan, yet I truly also bear all the names of my ancestors. But I can see that you did not come to hear that. Tell an old man what he may do for you.' You say that you have come to discover your own ancestors – those of your family and your race – and you ask Fintan to help you . . . He looks at you for a while in silence, then nods his head and bids you wait. He enters his hut and emerges again with a staff hung round with bells. He shakes this towards the west and in a moment, as if in answer, there comes the sound of galloping hooves. A white mare appears and Fintan bids you mount and go wherever she will take you. Then he whispers in her ear and she at once sets off at a great pace, her hooves pounding the earth like the steady beat of a great drum . . . As she gallops the white mare calls out to you, and you are not surprised to find that you can understand her. 'I am taking you to the first of your ancestors. Beyond that another will come.' The mare takes you to a hilltop where a group of lonely trees stand huddled in a rough circle, and there she stops. You get down from her back and see your own parents coming towards you. Now you are given the opportunity to learn from them. You may not always have agreed with them in the past; now you can speak clearly to them and you will find that they respect you and will answer you without anger or judgement. This is a moment in which you may also heal any wounds that may exist between you. Here in the Otherworld old enmities fall away, and even the greatest hurts can be bridged and spoken about with clarity and fairness. Take your time now and talk with your first ancestors . . .

PAUSE

After a time you become aware of the sound of swift hooves approaching. This time it is a great stag of many tines which comes to greet you. Once again you are able to understand its words. 'I am come to carry you to the next of your ancestors,' he says, and taking leave of your parents you climb onto his back and feel his powerful muscles bunch as he springs away down the hill and across an open landscape of rolling grassland . . . At length you arrive at a place where a great river courses through the plain, and there, waiting to greet you, are your grandparents. You may or may not remember them, but they know you, and have much to tell you of their time and your own family. Stay for a while and talk with them . . .

PAUSE

After a while you hear a snuffling and snorting approaching, and into sight comes a great bristly boar, whose red eyes shine with intelligence and who addresses you thus: 'I am come to lead you to your next ancestors.' You take leave of your grandparents and mount the huge hog's back. At once he begins to trot away, his hooves covering the ground with surprising speed . . . Soon you reach a woodland, and there waiting amid the trees are your great-grandparents . . . They may be no more than names to you, but they seem to know all about you and have much to tell . . . Spend some time with them and listen to what they have to say and teach you . . .

PAUSE

A little later you become conscious that a blackbird has been singing in the trees for some time, but now you hear that it is speaking to you. 'I have come to carry you to your next destination', it says, and as it flies down you see that either it has grown large, or you have become small enough to be carried on its back. You take leave of your great-grandparents and climb onto the bird's back . . . It takes flight at once and you are carried high above the land until you approach some low foothills leading to higher peaks beyond. Here the blackbird sets you down, and there, waiting to greet you, are your great-great-grandparents. Once again they seem to be expecting you, and you are given time to talk with them of their time and the wisdom they acquired in their lives . . .

PAUSE

In time you hear the harsh scream of an eagle, and there above you floats a bird of mighty proportions who cries that he has come to carry you to your next destination. You take leave of your great-great-grandparents and climb onto the bird's wide back. At once it flies off upwards towards the mountains, finally spiralling down to a sheltered place in the lea of some great rocks, where you find that your great-great-great-grandparents await you. They greet you with joy and you talk long of the knowledge they have gleaned from their time upon the earth . . .

PAUSE

This time it is the eagle who returns to fetch you. 'I have one further destination to take you,' he says, 'and that is to the oldest of the old, the Salmon which lives in the lake of Assaroe in the heights of these mountains. He will show you the rest of your history.' Mounting the eagle's back you are carried aloft again, waving down to your great-great-great-grandparents below. Soon you are set down beside a mountain tarn, the waters of which seem as black as the night sky. There, swimming to meet you, is the largest salmon you have ever seen. It puts its head out of the water and regards you with a single bright eye (the other is dim and sightless). 'You have seen further back along your own line of generation than many people,' he says. 'What more would you see? But take care, for I can show you only the truth, and this is not always what mortals require.' The time has come to ask of the salmon the question you have had in your mind from the start, though you may not have realized it. It is a question concerning your own heritage, which may take you far beyond the generations of a hundred, even a thousand years. It is to do with your own lineage and your part in the great story of creation. What you learn may indeed not be the answer you hoped to hear: it may tell you of other lands and other times, and it may help you to realize why you are who you are and why you are engaged upon this path of the shaman or shamanka. It may tell you of your own lands or of others with which you felt no special kinship. The answer may come in words or in visions; it may not be an easy one and you should be prepared for this before you ask the question. But once it is asked you *must* listen to the answer . . .

PAUSE

After a time which is outside time you are ready to take your leave of the salmon. You thank it for the words and the visions you received, and as it swims away you see approaching slowly along the shore of the tarn the ancient figure of Fintan. He greets you and asks if you are satisfied with what you have learned. 'You see now,' he says, 'what I meant when I said that I was the product of all the names I have borne. It is your task to honour your own ancestors and to discover more of what they can teach you.' Then he gently holds out his belled staff and shakes it before you. A door opens in the mountainside before you and you step through into your own world again. Record as much as you can remember of what you learned on this journey, for it will come to have great meaning for you in time to come.

STOKING WILD FIRES

The words which preface this chapter reflect the importance of ancestral wisdom and of keeping our traditions alive. If we neglect them they will die; it is as simple as that. If we want to go on working with and enjoying the benefits of our own native tradition we must work with it and live it *every day*. True shamanism can really only be learned in a tribal culture, from a shaman old in the ways of the art, with a deep understanding for and relationship to the land on which he or she was born. But this does not mean that shamanism cannot be practised by those who do not have access to such an immediate and physical teacher, or that it does not have a great deal to teach us today. We can still learn the teachings, adopt the philosophy and beliefs of the younger races of the world (by which I mean from an earlier time than ours), and we can grow and develop as a result.

I believe that the future of this old planet may well depend upon our relearning and re-establishing our shamanic roots, however far distant and fragmented they may be. The teachings we have shared through the pages of this book are the first steps towards understanding a heritage which belongs to us all.

Because this land was once Celtic. We have looked at shamanism through Celtic eyes. In this way we have been given the opportunity to perceive new dimensions and new possibilities, both for ourselves and for our world. As the shaman Antonio Morales remarks in Alberto Villoldo's book *The Four Winds*:

> The shaman . . . knows there is a sea of consciousness that is universal even though we each perceive it from our own shores, an awareness and a world that we all share, that can be experiencd by every being . . .

It is into that sea of consciousness, the Otherworld, that we have plunged again and again throughout this book. We have accompanied the Celtic shaman, asleep in his darkened cell of dreams, and watched him expel the darkness from within himself and set his soul aflame with the light of the stars. All who journey on this path of wholeness will find themselves, sooner or later, similarly transformed.

Appendix 1
The Mound of the World

When considering the Sacred Wheel, it is fascinating to examine additional evidence of a more solid nature. The Celts worshipped at sites which were open to the elements; they made use of ancient stone circles and standing stones, already established and planted circles of trees which represented, in microcosm, the universe they knew. Springs and rivers were also considered especially sacred as they rose in the Underworld and brought messages up to the Middleworld. Trees were conductors of energy, as were the so-called 'ley' lines, rivers of energy which formed a grid across the land. The shamans of the time would have known and worked from all such places, and today you can still derive great benefit from working at such power spots, although such practice is not essential. Working at or with an ancient site not only helps establish contact with the tradition, but also with an aspect of the self which is represented by the place – a kind of centre to which the apprentice shaman goes to extend his knowledge and where he feels secure.

However, it should never be forgotten that the indiscriminate use of such ancient sites is a major contribution to their demise. The constant draining of power by individuals and groups has stripped many of these places of their inherent power. Thus you should always give back something in exchange for what you take. The simple laying of a hand on one of the stones, or on the earth itself, is generally enough. Returning something of what has been received, as a freely given gift, is always a good thing. This does not mean that you will become drained; it is the willingness to make an offering to the sacred land, to give up the excess energy you may gain from working there, which is valuable.

A number of ancient mounds, scattered throughout the Celtic world, reflect this in a unique way. Known as 'long barrows', and for many years referred to as burial mounds, these have, in more recent times, been recognized as ritual places. Though built many hundreds of years before the Celts reached the British Isles, they were almost certainly used by the incoming people, in some cases taken over for their own ritual purposes. Celtic shamanism itself derives from long before the settling of the Indo-European tribes in Britain and Ireland. They too inherited an ancient system of belief and practice, which we may recognize in more than one kind of site.

The smaller barrows, of which there are literally hundreds scattered across England, Wales, Ireland and Scotland, represent a microcosm of creation. The dome of the building *above* the earth was mirrored by an exact echo *beneath* the earth. Small chambers lead off at each of the cardinal points, so that the resulting shape (though hidden to all but those with eyes to see) looked like this:

Perhaps we may also see more than an architectural design in the successive rings of corbelled stone. Each ring may have represented the levels of creation, rising about the Great Tree (a pole or tree-trunk set in the centre). Thus within the confines of such a place, as within the spirit lodges or hogans of the North American Indians, the shaman would have been able to act out his or her role as mediator between the worlds and the sacred powers of the wheel.

If we then look at a single example of a much larger mound, we will see how relevant these structures are to the practice of shamanism in Ireland and Britain.

New Grange is at the sacred centre of Ireland. It dates from Neolithic times, but figures largely in later Celtic accounts. From evidence found at the site we can conclude that shamanic ritual may have been carried out there over a long period of time, perhaps hundreds of years.

The mound itself, and its surrounding stone circle, form a perfect model of the cosmos. At one time there were thirty-five standing stones around the structure, which may be seen as a model of the *axis mundi*, or central mountain of the world. Within the mound the passage to the centre is divided by three massive stones, which mark off the transition between the three worlds (expressed vertically). To traverse them was to pass into the inner realms, where above/centre/below were recognized divisions.

The centre is an expression of the heart of Creation. Four small chambers, representing the four-fold division of the year (see Chapter 2) lead off on either side. Intricate carvings of spirals (a representation of the life-journey and the inspiration of initiation) cover the stones on

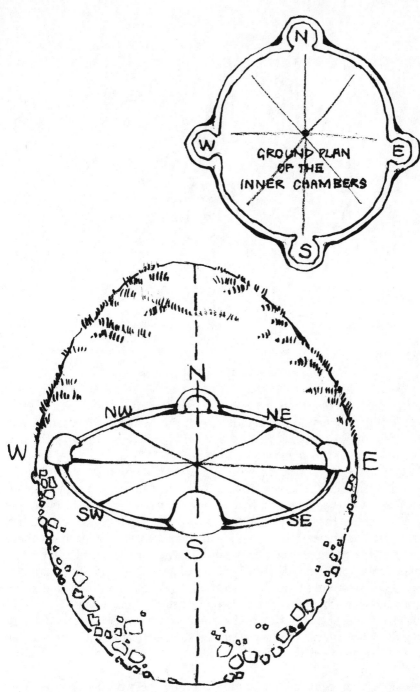

Figure 32. The Mound of the World

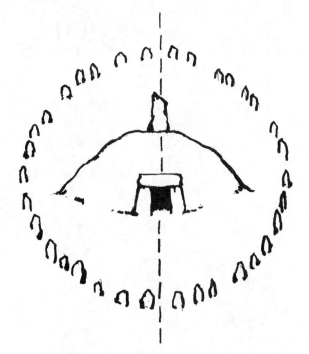

Figure 33. The Mound at New Grange

every side. At one time, as reported in a historical account of 1699, a great pillar stone stood above this point on the top of the mound, and this reinforces the belief that at one time a representation of the *axis mundi* stood at the centre of the mound.

Outside, the walls of the mound are faced with white quartz stones which sparkle in the sunlight. This is another expression of a constant theme in Celtic shamanism, that of passing from darkness to light. We may imagine the shaman, first entering the mound, passing within, through the three stages of the universe, pausing at each to make prayers and offerings, and finally reaching the darkened centre, where he experienced a profound vision, possibly induced by an initiatic drink of the kind referred to in the writings of Taliesin, or by some other consciousness-changing drug. Possibly the well documented entry of the sun, which strikes down the passage only once a year, on mid-winter's day, may have had a similarly revelatory effect. The shaman may have slept on the skin of a sacred animal, such as a bull, before waking and being brought forth into the dazzling light of day. At this point, having completed his inner journey, he would have given an inspired pronouncement concerning the life of the clan.

Such a ritual enactment can only be speculative, yet it is in keeping with the evidence from the site itself, and with the literature, mythology and folk-custom of the Celts, all of which embody material from a far more ancient period.

All of this is reflected in the making of the Sacred Wheel, and the taking of the Sacred Journey; the ancient uses are inherent not only at such sacred sites, but also in the modern circles of the practising shaman.

Appendix 2
The Grove of Knowledge

What kind of a shaman are you? Are you a healer? A warrior? A poet or musician? A seer or a seanachie? This exercise is designed to help you find out. It assumes that you have worked your way through the whole of this book and that you are now prepared to go out into the world as a working shaman or shamanka. You may already have a very good idea of what you want to do. If, however, you feel at all uncertain as to the direction in which you wish to go, the visualization which follows may help you to decide.

The Grove of Knowledge

As you prepare to enter the Grove of the Mysteries, which of old was known as Caer Gwydion, be aware of your place in the Circle of the World, and of your reasons for entering. For you have come to imbibe pure wisdom from the Masters of the Grove, to sit with Taliesin of the Radiant Brow and in time perhaps to sip from the Cauldron of Inspiration itself, which has long been kept here.

   With these things in mind, pass through the gates of the three worlds into the Grove of Forgetting and Remembering. See before you two great trees, ancient as the earth, and between them stretched a rainbow cloak of shifting, shimmering colours. Pass through this and reach a land of green hills and rich forest. It is night and a bright horned moon hangs in the black web of the sky. You are standing at the entrance to a grove of mighty trees which form a natural avenue leading ahead. Their spreading branches form a canopy high above your head, and the fallen leaves of centuries form a deep mast beneath your feet. As you progress deeper into the grove you see that the trees have been planted in ranks of different species. Oaks are the outermost bastion, the guardians of the grove; next are alder, and beyond them willow, ash and elm.

Then you find yourself emerging into a cleared space, surrounded by tall, slender birches. In the centre of the circle burns a great fire, and around it stand nine figures. One turns towards you and extends both hands, palms outward, fingers spread, in greeting. The firelight gleams on the slim circlet of silver about his brows. His hair and beard are carefully trimmed, and the colour of bronze. His eyes gleam brightly as he bows towards you. His robe is green, signifying that he is the Chief Poet of the Grove, and from this you know that he is Taliesin, the Radiant Browed, whose country is the Region of the Summer Stars.

He bids you step forward and names each of the nine men and women in turn. They are the Guardians of the Grove and their names may not be uttered aloud, but you hear them clearly with your inner hearing, and you will remember them at need.

Now Taliesin bids you look towards the centre of the circle, to where the fire burns brightly, and you see for the first time that a great cauldron hangs suspended over the blaze from an iron tripod. Ancient carvings decorate its sides and its rim is embellished with pearls. If you count them you will see how many there are. Then you hear the voice of the bard chanting:

> Perfect is the Cauldron of the Goddess
> In the Sanctuary of Spendid Song.
> My tongue is freed in her presence.
> To whom is offered milk, and dew, and acorns.
> See where the cauldron shines
> In the firmament of the heavens.
> In the Court of Arianrhod
> In the Circle of the Stars.

Raising your eyes you see in the night sky, beyond the silver circlet of the moon, a pattern of stars, the Northern Crown, glowing with brilliant light. Between them, you seem to see the outlines of another cauldron, greater by far than its humble, earthly representation. Transparent, outlined in stars from whose light they seem fashioned, you see nine beautiful women around the cauldron, their breath, streaming out like silver mist, warming its rim. Faint but clear comes the sound of voices raised in a song of unearthly beauty which touches you and awakens deep longing to achieve your intention in coming to this place . . .

Again you hear the voice of Taliesin, speaking of your vocation to the world. There are, he tells you, many different kinds of shaman, and of these nine are represented here: the seanachie, or story-teller; the poet; the healer; the seer; the brehon, or law-giver; the hunter; the smith; the shaman and the warrior. He asks, which of these paths will you follow and bids you walk a while in silence and consider your answer.

With these words in your ears you begin to walk the circle of the grove, with eyes cast down and thoughts turned inward, focusing upon your reasons for coming to this sacred place and what you will attempt to do in the world with what you have learned and will learn. Taliesin walks with you. If you wish you may speak with him and question him concerning what you have seen and heard, or upon any other matter that lies near your heart.

Around the grove the eight remaining figures stand, silent in their rainbow robes. As you pass, each one holds out a symbol of his or her skill. You see a silver branch, sign of the story-teller; a crystal in the hands of the healer; a wooden disc with a spiral for the seer; a hazel staff for the brehon; a bow for the hunter; a hammer for the smith; a spear for the warrior; a bag for the shaman. In Taliesin's hands is the symbol of his office, the harp.

Before each one you hesitate. Is this your way? If you wish you may question the guardians. Some will offer you challenges and these you should accept. Try your new skills against these mighty ones, discover for yourself what you are capable of . . .

After a time, which is no time in this grove, you pause again before one of the guardians. This is the role you have chosen for yourself . . . take the symbol of your innermost skill from its master or mistress and place it in your own shamanic crane-bag. Then take leave of the Guardians of the Grove of Knowledge. As you prepare to depart you hear voices of nine, lead by Taliesin, upraised in a song praising the wonders of the cauldron:

> We praise the One
> who in our heads
> set soul and reason,
> who, to keep guard over us
> bestowed our seven senses –
> from fire and earth, water and air,
> from mist and flowers,
> from wind and trees,
> much skilful wisdom
> is bestowed upon us.

Gradually, the voices grow faint, and with it the leaping firelight grows dim, and the tall sentinel trees fade away. Slowly you become aware of your own place and time and open your eyes. Whatever decision you have made on this journey will be of the utmost importance to you in the time to come. You have awoken the shaman within. Your tasks lie before you.

Bibliography

There are no books about Celtic shamanism as such, though many conventional studies of Celtic lore and life deal with aspects of the subject. Therefore the majority of books about shamanism listed here deal with North American, Aboriginal, Saxon or Siberian aspects. These are well worth reading by the serious student, for the very clear parallels which will soon be appreciated beneath the various cultural differences. Titles marked thus * have been especially useful in the writing of this book.

Basilov, V.N. 'The Shaman Drum Among the Peoples of Siberia' in *Traces of the Central Asian Cultue in the North*, Ed by I. Lehtinen etc, Toimituksia, 1986.

Bassett, M.G. *Formed Stones, Folklore & Fossils*, National Museum of Wales, 1982.

Bathurst, W. *Roman Antiquities at Lydney Park, Gloucestershire*, Spottiswoode & Co. 1897.

Beck, P.V., Walters, A.L., and Francisco, N., *The Sacred*, Navahjo Community College Press, 1990.

Berry, W. *Standing on Earth*, Golgonooza Press, 1991.

Best, R.I. 'Prognostications from the Raven and the Wren', *Eriu* VIII (1916), pp120–6; see pp123–5.

Best, R.I. 'The Settling of the Manor of Tara', *Eriu* IV (1910), pp121–172.

Bloom, W. *Sacred Times: A New Approach to Festivals*, Findhorn Press, 1990.

Brennan, M. *The Boyne Valley Vision*, The Dolmen Press, 1980.

Bromwich, R. (ed and trans) *Trioedd Ynys Prydein (The Welsh Triads)*, University of Wales Press, 1978.

Bruford, A. *Gaelic Folk-Tales & Medieval Romances*, Folklore of Ireland Society, 1969.

*Cahill, S. and Halpern, J. *The Ceremonial Circle: Shamanic Practice, Ritual & Renewal*, Mandala, 1991.

Calder, G. *Auriacept Na N-Eces* (The Scholar's Primer), John Grant, 1917.

*Capps, W.H. (ed) *Seeing with a Native Eye*, Harper & Row, 1977.

Carey, John, 'Suibne Geilt and Tuan mac Cairill' in *Eigse*, Vol. 20 (1984), pp93–105.

Carmichael, A. *Carmina Gadelica*, Scottish Academic Press, 1928–1972.

Cary, J. 'Nodons in Britain & Ireland' in *Zeitschrift für Celtische Philologie*, Vol 40 (1984), pp1–22.

Chadwick, N.K. 'Dreams in Early European Literature' in *Celtic Studies*, Ed J. Carney & D. Greene, Routledge & Kegan Paul, 1968, p38.

Cross, T.P. and C.H, Slover (eds) *Ancient Irish Tales*, Figgis, 1936.

Davidson, J. *The Formative Mind*, Element Books, 1991.

Doore, G. (ed) *Shaman's Path*, Shambhala, 1988.

Eliade, M. *Images & Symbols*, Princetown University Press, 1991.

Eliade, M. *Shamanism*, Princetown University Press, 1972.

Ereira, A. *The Heart of the World*, Cape, 1991.

Ettlinger, Ellen 'Omens and Celtic Warfare' in *Man* XLIII (1943), No 4, pp11–17; see pp11–12.

Ettlinger, Ellen 'Precognitive Dreams in Celtic Legend' in *FolkLore* LIX (1948), pp97–111.

Forbes, A.R. *Gaelic Names of Beasts, Birds, Fishes, Insects & Reptiles*, Oliver & Boyd, 1905.

Ford, Patrick K. 'The Well of Nechtan' and 'La Gloire Luminesse' in *Myth in Indo-European Antiquity*, ed G.J. Larson, University of California Press (1974), pp67–74.

Gantz, J. *Early Irish Myths and Sagas*, Penguin Books, 1981.

Gantz, J. (ed & trans) *The Mabinogion*, Penguin Books, 1976.

Goodman, F. 'Body Posture and the Religious Altered State of Consciousness' in *Journal of Humanistic Psychology* 26 (1986), pp81–118.

*Goodman, F. *Where the Spirits Ride the Wind: Trance Journeys and Other Ecstatic Experiences*, Indiana University Press, 1990.

*Gose, E.B. *The World of the Irish Wonder Tale*, University of Toronto Press, 1985.

Graves, R. *The White Goddess*, Faber, 1952.

Green, M. *Symbol and Image in Celtic Religious Art*, Routledge, 1989.

Grim, J. *Reflections on Shamanism*, Teilhard Studies No 6., American Teilhard Association, 1981.

Grof, C. and S. *The Stormy Search for the Self*, Mandala, 1991.

Hart, M. and Stevens, J. *Drumming at the Edge of Magic*, Harper-Collins, 1991.

Hedges, J.W. *Tomb of the Eagles: A Window on Stone Age Tribal Britain*, John Murray, 1984.

Hersh, J. 'Ancient Celtic Incubation' in *Sundance Community Dream Journal* III (Winter, 1979), pp81–90.

Highwater, J. *The Primal Mind*, New American Library, 1981.

Hull, Eleanor, 'The Hawk of Achill or the Legend of the Oldest Animals' in *Folklore* Vol 43 (1932), pp376–409.

Ingerman, S. *Soul Retrieval: Mending the Fragmented Self Through Shamanic Practice*, Harper, 1991.

Jackson, K.H. *A Celtic Miscellany*, Routledge & Kegan Paul, 1951.

Janhunen, J. 'Siberian Shamanistic Terminology' in *Traces of the Central Asian Culture in the North*, ed I. Lehtinen, Toimiyuksia, 1986.

Jones, P. and Matthews, C. *Voices from the Circle*, Aquarian Press, 1990.

Joyce, P.W. *A Social History of Ancient Ireland*, Longmans, 1903.

*King, S.K. *Urban Shaman*, Simon & Schuster, 1990.

Kinsella, T. *The Tain*, Dolmen Press, 1969.

Krippner, S. 'Dreams and Shamanism' in *Shamanism* compiled by S. Nicholson, The Theosophical Publishing House, 1987.

LaChapelle, D. *Sacred Land, Sacred Sex: The Rapture of the Deep*, Finn Hill Arts, 1988.

Loffler, C.M. *The Voyage to the Otherworldly Island in Early Irish Literature*, Institut für Anglistik und Amerikanistik der Universität Saltzburg, 1983.

Lonsdale, S. *Animals & the Origins of Dance*, Thomas & Hudson, 1981.

*Lorler, M. *Shamanic Healing within the Medicine Wheel*, The Brotherhood of Life, 1989.

Macallister, R.A.S. *The Secret Languages of Ireland*, Amorica Book Co. 1976.

Mac Cana, P. *The Learned Tales of Medieval Ireland*, Dublin Institute for Advanced Studies, 1980.

McKay, J.G. 'The Deer-Cult & the Deer Goddess Cult of the Ancient Caledonians, in *Folk-Lore* XLIII (1932), pp144–74.

Mails, T.E. *Fools Crow: Wisdom & Power*, Council Oak Books, 1991.

Mason, B.S. *How to Make Drums, Tomtoms and Rattles*, Dover Publications, 1974.

*Matthews, C. *The Celtic Book of the Dead*, St Martin's Press, 1992.

*Matthews, C. *Elements of the Celtic Tradition*, Element Books, 1990.

Matthews, C. *Mabon and the Mysteries of Britain*, Arkana, 1987.

Matthews, J. 'Auguries, Dreams & Incubatory Sleep' in *Psychology & the Spiritual Traditions*, R.J. Stewart, Element Books, 1990.

Matthews, J. *Elements of the Arthurian Tradition*, Element Books, 1990.

*Matthews, J. *Song of Taliesin: Stories of A Shaman*, Aquarian, 1991.

*Matthews, J. *Taliesin: Shamanism and the Bardic Mysteries in Britain and Ireland*, Aquarian Press, 1991.

Matthews, J. and C. *The Western Way* (2 vols), Arkana, 1985–6.

Medicine Grizzlybear Lake, *Native Healer*, Quest Books, 1991.

Meier, C.A. 'Ancient Incubation and Modern Psychotherapy' in *Betwixt & Between*, ed by L.C. Mahdi, S. Foster & M. Little, Open Court, 1987.

*Meier, C.A. *Healing Dream & Ritual*, Daimon, 1989.

Meyer, K. (ed & trans) *The Voyage of Bran*, David Nutt, 1895.

Mikhailovskii, V.M. 'Shamanism in Siberia and European Russia' in *Journal of the Royal Archaeological Institute of Great Britain and Ireland* 24 (1894), pp62–100, 126–158.

Murphy, G. (ed & trans) *Duanaire Finn*, Irish Text Society, 1953.

Naddair, K. *Celtic Folk and Faery Tales*, Rider Books, 1989.

Nagy, J.F. 'Otter, Salmon & Eel in Traditional Gaelic Narrative' in *The Celtic Review* 20–23 (1985/8), pp123–144.

Neihardt, J.G. *Black Elk Speaks*, University of Nebraska, 1979.

Nicholson, S. (ed) *Shamanism*, Theosophical Publishing House, 1987.

Noel, D.C. 'Archetypal Merlin & the New Shamanism' in *Psychology & the Spiritual Traditions*, ed R.J. Stewart, Element Books, 1990.

O'Curry, E. (ed & trans) 'The Sick-Bed of Cuchulainn and the Only Jealousy of Emer' in *The Atlantis* IV (1863), pp98–124.

O'Hogain, D. *Myth, Legend, and Romance: An Encyclopaedia of the Irish Folk Traditions*, Ryan Publishing, 1990.

O'Suilleabhain, M. *The Bodhran: A Practical Introduction*, Walton's Musical Instrument Galleries, 1984.

Pintar, J. *A Voice From the Earth: the Cards of Winds & Changes*, Mandala, 1990.

Purcell, B. 'Newgrange: Between Sun and Stone' in *The Crane Bag* Vol 2. Nos 1&2 (1978), pp89–95.

Rees, A. & B. *Celtic Heritage*, Thames & Hudson, 1961.

Rees, I.G. 'Totem Beasts and Therapeutic Counselling' in *Psychology and the Spiritual Traditions*, ed R.J. Stewart, Element Books, 1990.

Rhys, John, *Celtic Folk-Lore, Welsh & Manx*, Wildwood House, 1980.

Ritchie, A. 'Painted Pebbles in Northern Scotland' in *Antiquaries of Scotland* Vol 104 (1972), pp297–301.

Sharp, E.A. *Lyra Celtica*, Patrick Geddes, 1896.

Sikes, W. *British Goblins: the Realm of Faery*, Llanerch Publishers, 1991.

Smyth, D. *A Guide to Irish Mythology*, Irish Academic Press, 1988.

Spaan, D.B. *The Otherworld in Early Irish Literature*, University of Michigan, 1969.

*Stevens, J. & L. *Secrets of Shamanism*, Avon Books, 1988.

Stewart, R.J. *Celtic Gods, Celtic Goddesses*, Blandford Press, 1990.

Stewart, R.J. 'Spiritual Animals, Guardians, Guides and Other Places in *Psychology & the Spiritual Traditions*, ed R.J. Stewart, Element Books, 1990.

*Swann, J.A. *Sacred Places: How the Living Earth Seeks our Friendship*, Bear & Co, 1990.

Thomas, N. L. *Irish Symbols of 3500 BC*, The Mercier Press, 1988.

Vastokas, J.M. 'The Shamanic Tree of Life' in *Artscanasda* nos 184–187 (1973/4), pp125–49.

*Villoldo, A. and Jendresen, E. *The Four Winds: A Shaman's Odyssey into the Amazon*, Harper & Row, 1990.

Walters, F. *Book of the Hopi*, Penguin Books, 1977.

Wheeler, R.E.M. *Report on the Excavations of the Prehistoric, Roman and Post-Roman Site in Lydney Park, Gloucestershire*, Oxford: Society of Antiquaries (1932), pp51–2.

*Wood-Martin, W.G. *Traces of the Elder Faiths of Ireland*, Longmans, 1902.

Ywahoo, D. *Voices of Our Ancestors*, Shambhala, 1987.

Resources

DRUMS AND OTHER CRAFTS

Berkana
39 Randisbourne Gardens
Bellingham
Lughdunum, (London) SE6 3BS
UK

Bodhrans and other kinds of drums
and Celtic artwork.

Eagle Craft Bodhrans
A. & S. Roberts
Corner Cottage
6 Green Lane
Eastburn
Nr Keighley
West Yorkshire BD20 8UT

English goatskin bodhrans with
hand-painted Celtic designs.

Alawn Tickhill
Galdraheim
35 Wilson Avenue
Deal
Kent CT14 9NL

Produces an excellent catalogue of
shamanic tools and artefacts.

Coranieid Crafts
14 Richmond Road
Swanage
Dorset BH19 2PZ

Produce a catalogue of bodhrans
and other Celtic crafts.
Excellent workmanship.

Pathways
28 Cowl Street
Evesham
Worcs WR11 4PL

Courses on making frame drums
from native British materials.
Emphasis on native American
teachings of the Medicine Wheel,
but still the best drums I have
found.

IMAGES

Chesca Potter.
PO Box 196
London WC1A 2DY

Images of Celtic gods and goddesses.

Courtney Davies
St Just-in-Cornwall Ltd
6E Lang Rock Industrial Estate
Penzance
Cornwall TR20 8HX

Images of Celtic gods and goddesses, Celtic designs and much
more.

Stuart Littlejohn
1 Gosses Cottages
Crediton
Devon

Images of Celtic gods and goddesses.

Miranda Gray
41 Lodge Rd
Portswood
Southampton
Hants SO2 0RL

Images of Celtic gods and goddesses. Illustrations from *The Arthurian Tarot* cards etc.

JOURNALS

Shaman's Drum
PO Box 430
Willits
CA 95490
USA

The best journal on world shamanism.

Medicine Ways
35 Wilson Avenue
Deal
Kent CT14 9NL

The only native British shamans'
magazine to date.

TAPES

Robin Williamson
BCM 4797
London WC1N 3XX

5 Celtic Tales of Enchantment
5 Legendary Histories of Britain
5 Bardic Mysteries
*5 Humorous Tales of Scotland and
Ireland*

And many more of the best in Celtic music and storytelling by a modern bard. Write to the above address for list and details of forthcoming tours.

Nigel Shaw
Spiral Publications
8 King Street
Glastonbury
Somerset BA6 9JY

Good meditation music with a Celtic/Arthurian slant.

OGHAM

Turning Trees: An Ogham Stick Game
Hernan Turner
Killoughter Rd
Galway
Ireland

A useful and instructive way to learn ogham.

The Celtic Tree Oracle by Liz and Colin Murray (Rider Books, 1988)

Book and card set. A divinatory system derived from the Celtic free alphabet.

ORGANIZATIONS

Foundation for Shamanic Studies
(USA)
Box 670
Belden Station
Norwalk
CT 06852

(Europe)
Scandinavian Centre for Shamanic Studies
Jonathan Horowitz & Annette Host
Artellerivej 63/140
DK–2300
Kobenhavn
Sweden

(UK)
Bella Holliday
Ivy Dene
124 North Road
Middle Barton
Oxford OX5 4DA

Courses worldwide on the Harner
Method of shamanism.

International Conference on Shamanism and Healing
2321 Russell ST, '3A
Berkeley
CA 94705
USA

TAPES

John & Caitlín Matthews
Shamanising: A Tape especially manufactured to go with this book will be available shortly; all enquiries to the address below. As well as this we also produce tapes to accompany our workshops and produce a quarterly newsletter. Please send four first-class stamps if in the UK or Europe, or eight international postage reply paid coupons if outside Europe, to: BCM Hallowquest, London, WC1N 3XX.
The other tapes are: *Celtic Shamanism*; *Poems of Taliesin*; *Celtic Dialogues*; *Shamanic Singing Journey*. These are not professionally recorded, but are useful adjuncts to learning.

Michael Harner
Foundation for Shamanic Studies (see under 'Organizations' for address): *Course in Shamanism* (four tapes); *Singing Journey for Shamanic Voyaging*; *Drumming for the Shamanic Journey*; *Singing Bow for the Shamanic Journey*.

Kenneth Meadows
Shamanic Experience
Available from: Element Books
Longmead
Shaftesbury
Dorset SP7 8PL

R. J. Stewart
Journey to the Underworld; *Music Power Harmony*; *Magical Songs*; *More Magical Songs*; *Advanced Magical Arts* (three tapes). Tapes of music, chanting and visualization. Concerts by arrangement.
Tapes available from:
Element Books
Longmead
Shaftesbury
Dorset SP7 8PL

Index